Why You Lose At Poker

Russell Fox

Scott T. Harker

Other ConJelCo titles by Russell Fox and Scott T. Harker:

Mastering No-Limit Hold'em

Other ConJelCo books:

Cooke's Rules of Real Poker
by Roy Cooke and John Bond

Hold'em Excellence
by Lou Krieger

The Home Poker Handbook
by Roy Cooke and John Bond

Internet Poker
by Lou Krieger and Kathleen Keller Watterson

The Mathematics of Poker
by William Chen and Jerrod Ankenman

More Hold'em Excellence
by Lou Krieger

Real Poker II: The Play of Hands
by Roy Cooke and John Bond

Real Poker III: The Best of Cooke 1992-2005
by Roy Cooke and John Bond

Serious Poker
by Dan Kimberg

Stepping Up
by Randy Burgess

Winning Low-Limit Hold'em
by Lee Jones

Winning Omaha/8 Poker
by Mark Tenner and Lou Krieger

Video Poker—Optimum Play
by Dan Paymar

Software

Blackjack Trainer for the Macintosh or Windows
Ken Elliott's CrapSim for DOS
StatKing for Windows

Why You Lose At Poker

Russell Fox

Scott T. Harker

ConJelCo
Pittsburgh, Pennsylvania

Why You Lose At Poker
Copyright © 2006 by Russell Fox and Scott T. Harker

Publisher's Cataloging-in-Publication Data

Fox, Russell
Harker, Scott T.

Why You Lose At Poker/Fox/Harker.
viii, 212 p. 22 cm.

ISBN-10 1-886070-26-1
ISBN-13 978-1-886070-26-4

I. Title.

Library of Congress Control Number: 2006924664

First Edition

3 5 7 9 8 6 4

Cover design by Cat Zaccardi
Edited by Michael Patterson

ConJelCo LLC
1460 Bennington Ave.
Pittsburgh, PA 15217-1139
[412] 621-6040
http://www.conjelco.com

Table of Contents

Acknowledgements

In August 2005 we were sitting in the poker room at the Plaza Hotel in Las Vegas talking about our first book, *Mastering No-Limit Hold'em*. We were attending B.A.R.G.E. (Big August Rec Gambling Excursion; see http://www.barge.org for more information about this annual gathering), the most fun a poker player can have. As we were shooting the breeze, our good friend Peter Secor walked up and asked us what we were planning on writing next.

We had been tossing around several ideas but we were uncertain about what would be best to attempt. Peter mentioned a bridge book titled *Why You Lose at Bridge*. This book, by S. J. Simon, remains in print today, forty years from its first printing (you'll find it listed in our bibliography). It's a classic, in every sense of the word.

We read *Why You Lose at Bridge* (one of us is a tournament bridge player and understood everything in the book while the other read it just for the style). We came to the conclusion that there was nothing like this book in the poker world, and that it was just begging to be written.

So thank you, Peter Secor. This book would not have happened without you, because the authors would never have met without B.A.R.G.E. being in existence; Peter and our publisher, Chuck Weinstock, organize B.A.R.G.E. each year. And second, thanks for planting the seed of an excellent idea.

Scott:

This book is dedicated to my wife, Brittania. No woman on the planet could have been more understanding and forgiving than you have been over the last six months. Thank you for tolerating those endless nights on the other side of my closed office door. You are my angel, my muse, and my one true love.

Russ:

I especially want to thank my brother, Brett. He has been of tremendous support over the last several years as I was building my business and wondering whether it would succeed.

Both:

We chose Michael "mickdog" Patterson as our editor for our first book. He is a close friend to us both, and a wonderful editor. It was only natural that we ask him to assist us with our second effort, and we couldn't be more pleased. Thanks for the great job, Mick! You're the best! We would also like to thank David Heller for his help in correcting the second printing.

Foreword

Let's get the inevitable trash talk out of the way. You may be thinking, "Why am I not surprised that Andy Bloch wrote the foreword to *Why You Lose At Poker?*" To those of you who are thinking that, why am I not surprised that *you're* reading this book? Russell and Scott (the authors) are friends and when they asked me to write this foreword, I said "sure, but why am I not surprised that you two are writing this book?"

Actually, Russell and Scott are great poker writers and may also be marketing geniuses. You might be ashamed to buy this book for yourself (you shouldn't be), but it's the perfect poker gift to buy someone else. The title is also sure to set itself apart from the gazillion poker books that have come out in the last few years. Search Amazon for books with "poker" and "win" or "winning" in the title, and you'll find 157 books. Search for "poker" and "lose" or "losing" and you'll find three (besides this book) — one about video poker, and two that are over 10 years old and out of print. Every book wants to talk about winning; it's time for a book to talk about losing.

I've been a professional poker player for about 10 years. I've gone through the inevitable losing streaks. I don't let them get me down, but I don't ignore the losses. I use them as opportunities to improve my game. Whether I win or lose, I'm constantly looking at my own play and thinking about whether I could have played better.

One of the perks I get as part of "Team Full Tilt" (the group of top players who represent the on line poker site Full Tilt Poker) is access to the other members of the team. I get to exchange ideas with players like Phil Ivey, Chris Ferguson, Howard Lederer, and Erik Seidel, and hear how they've become the great players that they are.

Although they have different styles, what they all have in common is their constant thirst to improve their games. Even after they win a major poker championship, what they're thinking about is how bad they played, even if it's only one hand. They almost always think that they could have played better.

Sure, even after seven WSOP bracelets, Erik Seidel will never forget how he played the final hand of the 1988 World Series against Johnny Chan, the movie Rounders made sure of that. That's not surprising, because he lost. It's also not surprising that Chris Ferguson questions the play he made to win the WSOP in 2000—he was behind when he called, and had a 9 not hit on the river to save his A9 against TJ Cloutier's AQ, Cloutier would have had a commanding lead. But talk to them after they played masterfully to win a major tournament, and the first thing you're likely to hear from a player like Ivey or Ferguson is how badly they played a hand or two.

All of these players also went through periods of losing at the start of their poker learning, and they haven't forgotten. Howard Lederer was practically living in a poker club in NYC, picking up a few dollars a day cleaning and running errands, then losing the money every night at the low limit tables. His sister Katy even wrote about it in her memoir *Poker Face*. Sure, we were all embarrassed about our losing periods, but by admitting to ourselves that we were losers we were able to figure out the reasons and change. Now we can look back at our losing periods with pride, because it shows us how far we've come.

I remember back in 1993 when I started playing casino poker regularly, and I first played 1-5-5-10 limit at a Wednesday night home poker game in Boston. The talk of the game's email list that week (before I was added) was how this new player Bloch was such a big fish. I knew the reason I lost was poor play, not because I was unlucky. Analyzing my play, I realized the mistakes I made were like most mistakes, causing me to lose more money on bad hands, not failing to win money with my good hands. By concentrating at first on minimizing losing plays one at a time, I was able to start winning by my third or fourth week in the game. A few weeks later, I won a $100 buy-in no-limit tournament at Foxwoods, the first time I played no-limit, and at the next Wednesday night game of course I wore my winner's jacket.

The key to my dramatic turnaround was recognizing that I was trying too hard to win too often. Even the greatest baseball hitters don't try to swing at every pitch—you shouldn't be trying to win every pot, or even every time you start with good cards. You have to be willing to lose hands if you want to win in the long run. Otherwise, you'll convince yourself every hand that you have enough pot odds or implied odds to keep playing and you'll get destroyed. The most crucial aspect of winning poker is learning how to lose no more than you have to. If you learn why you lose at poker, you'll learn how to win.

Andy Bloch
Las Vegas, NV
May, 2006

Introduction

Why did we write this book?

To make money, of course!

Actually, we're writing this book to help *you* lose less money. Of course, that's what every poker book written is supposed to do, but this book is a little different. See, one afternoon not so long ago, we were discussing certain aspects of poker books, and what made the good ones good and the other ones, well, not so good. It turns out that almost every poker book has at least two or three good ideas. Even the books we don't think are worth the money will include at least some little nugget that will make you (or save you) money at the poker table.

One of the ways that we've found to improve our poker game is to focus on one problem area (some might call them "holes" or "leaks" in your game) at a time. Concentrating on only one aspect of your game, either while you play or while you're away from the tables, will help you plug that leak. And of course, the more leaks you plug, the more watertight your game will be.

So we thought, what if the biggest leaks were all listed in one book? How cool would it be to write a book that listed all of the major reasons why people lose money playing poker? Every poker book lists a few, but no poker book mentions all of them. Of course, there are many little holes in any player's game. Over time, all those little holes can create some serious leakage. But we thought that if we focused on the fifteen or so biggest problem areas in a typical poker player's game, we'd really have something worth reading.

So, we set out to create our list. Needless to say, we came up with a lot more than fifteen. In fact, we came up with over forty! Yet, with some careful study, we discovered that most of these problem areas fit into sixteen general categories. That made it easy.

Now before you think you've discovered poker's version of the Fountain of Youth, let us say a few things.

First, there is very little new material in this book. You won't find any profound revelations or "secrets the pros don't want you to know." Much of what we've written here has been written several times over in one version or another. You won't find any cool systems showing you how to win tournaments, nor will you find a complete explanation of game theory or inflection points. We'll leave that to the math guys and tournament experts. In fact, we've listed some further reading that we'd recommend to continue your never-ending poker education. You'll find that in Appendix B.

What you will find here is a simple, easy to read and understand guide to the biggest reasons why people lose at poker. We're not trying to set the poker world ablaze with controversial strategies and over-the-top moves that will have the WPT crowds oooing and ahhing. We've simply written a book to assist you in identifying your problem areas and show you how to take care of them, one at a time.

It's in the Numbers

One thing you're going to have to face is the reality of the math behind poker. And before you start to close this book, put it back on the shelf and reach for another one to buy, read on.

Poker math, as we'll explain, is not at all difficult. We'll discuss math in most of the chapters you'll be reading, and by the end of the book, you'll have a much better understanding of how the math of poker and a player's lack of its understanding is one of the most important topics we'll cover.

The math of poker involves simple addition, subtraction, multiplication and division. That's it. Any calculation you need to make at the table can be done with third grade math skills. And the best part is, once you get used to making these simple calculations, they become easier with time. Trust us.

One of your authors (we won't say which one as he'd be rather embarrassed) is, shall we say, not a natural when it comes to numbers. There's nothing wrong with that. Some of us have an aptitude for math, while others have an aptitude for the written word. But with math as simple as we're about to show you, you've got nothing to worry about, regardless of your ability to juggle numbers. For a quick course on the math of poker, review Appendix A.

The Rest is in Understanding

How long have you been playing poker? A week? A year? Fifty years? And how much do you understand—and we mean *really* understand—about poker? Are you honest enough with yourself to admit that you're losing money and you don't know why?

It's always the first step, and it's the toughest. If you're not making money playing poker, and if you want to become a winning player, eventually you're going to have to admit (at least to yourself) that there are certain things about poker that you just don't understand. It must be the case, or you wouldn't have purchased this book. In fact, just the purchase of this book is an admission that you don't understand everything there is to learn about the game of poker. And that's good, because here's a little secret for you: we don't understand everything either.

All winning players, from the $30-$60 hold'em pros grinding it out every day to the flamboyant characters you see tearing up the tournament trail, have one thing in common: they've all been in your shoes. Every single one of them has had to admit at one time or another that they just didn't understand certain aspects of poker. We certainly had to. In fact, we make it a point to try to learn and understand something new every time we play the game. There comes a moment in almost every session of poker when we just don't understand why someone made a play that he did, or how some things always seem to occur. We've made it our life's mission to figure it all out.

It is this lack of understanding that costs poker players money. And our goal in writing this book is to give you a great head start in understanding just why, *oh why*, you lose at poker.

Chapter Breakdown

For those of you who have read our first book, *Mastering No-Limit Hold'em*, the first thing you'll notice about this book is that it's written in a much more relaxed and casual style. We believe it's easier to learn certain things in a relaxed setting, and we've done our best in this book to help you unwind and have fun while you learn.

In fact, we've also given you some friends to take the journey with you. Ten of them, to be exact. And they're all different. A couple are good players, some are average players, and a couple are just rotten. Oh, and then there's Mrs. Goldman. You'll get to know her in a little bit, and you'll see why she's in a class all by herself.

We'll take these chapters one at a time, and we've written them in such a way that you can easily study one chapter for a while until you are comfortable with the concepts in it before heading on to the next.

We recommend you read the whole book, of course, but if you come to a chapter that you feel is just review for you, go ahead and jump to the next one. You can always come back to those chapters you've skipped and refresh your poker education when needed.

Chapter 2 – The Money You Lose Playing Too Many Hands. We start off with the most common error in poker. If you are losing money on a regular basis, chances are, you're not folding nearly enough. If you think J8o or A6s are fine hands to play in third position, this is a chapter you need to read . . . *now!*

Chapter 3 – The Money You Lose By Not Taking the Initiative. Has anyone told you that aggression is the key to poker? Have you noticed that the players who are usually betting and raising are the ones with the big stacks in front of them? There's a reason for that. We'll tell you all about it, and why you need to be the attacker and not the defender.

Chapter 4 – The Money You Lose By Not Recognizing When You're Beat. Have you ever been involved in a poker hand and found yourself tossing chips into the pot with that feeling that you were never going to see them again? Actually, that's a good sign, since it shows that you at least have an idea of when you are behind. Learn to recognize those situations and you'll save countless bets every session.

Chapter 5 – The Money You Lose By Not Considering Your Opponents. If you're playing against every opponent in the same fashion, you're making a terrible mistake—a lot of mistakes, in fact. We'll show you how certain plays work against only some opponents and when a completely different strategy is called for based on the tendencies of the players sitting at your table.

Chapter 6 – The Money You Lose Making Incorrect Bet Sizes in "Big Bet" Games. There are many books written on limit poker—especially limit hold'em. And there are very few books written on big-bet poker (pot-limit and no-limit). For this reason, most players new to big-bet poker have no understanding of proper bet sizes. And it costs them plenty.

Chapter 7 – The Money You Lose With Poor Bluffing Habits. Someone once said, "The bluff is king." Well, that may or may not be true, but if you don't know how or when to bluff, it might as well be the court jester. We show you why certain bluffs work while others backfire, often with disastrous results.

Chapter 8 – The Money You Lose By Making Mechanical Errors. Have you ever checked when you meant to bet? Have you ever acted out of turn? Have you ever "mis-clicked" in an online poker game? Sure you have. We all have. Here are some of the most common mechanical errors and how to avoid making them. You will not only save yourself some embarrassment, but potentially some money as well.

Chapter 9 – The Money You Lose Playing for Only Half the Pot. If you enjoy split pot games such as Omaha high-low and stud high-low, you really need to read this chapter. Find out why the hands you need to be most concerned with are those that have the potential to scoop an entire pot, and not just win half. This one chapter alone could be the key to winning in these enjoyable and profitable games.

Chapter 10 – Losing Because You Can't Handle Money. As odd as that might sound, most people are not prepared to monetarily handle the game of poker. Whether it's playing in a game too high for your bankroll, playing with money that should be used for other things, or playing scared because losing would hurt too much, you need to understand the importance of proper bankroll and money issues *before you play.*

Chapter 11 – Losing Because You Shouldn't Be Playing. Like it or not, your personal life can greatly impact your poker playing ability. If you're drunk, sad, tired, sick, worried, angry... well, you get the picture. Perhaps it's not a good time to play. We show you why it's so important to be focused and ready to play, and why sometimes you should just stay home.

Chapter 12 – Losing Because You're Not Properly Educated. In the days of Texas Dolly, Sailor, and the Grand Old Man, poker books were scarce and virtually unheard of. Players had to learn by experience alone. But you're lucky. With an amazing array of books, videos, discussion groups and coaches available to everyone, we explain why it's so important to study the game away from the table as well as at it.

Chapter 13 – Losing Because You Don't Understand the Math of Poker. Don't fret. We're going to have some fun. We talk about simple poker math and how to figure out if you should call, raise or fold. We tell you all about odds and outs and why calculating them is just as easy as it is important.

Chapter 14 – Losing Because You're Playing in Tournaments. Yeah, we know they are fun, but we show you why you're not winning as often as you think you should. The math behind poker tournaments is guaranteed to surprise you. Give this chapter a read before you buy in to your next tournament. You might think twice.

Chapter 15 – Losing Because of Bad Luck. No, blaming your losses on bad luck isn't always another sorry excuse. Poker is still gambling, and luck (good or bad) can strike at any time. We explain what's happening (yes, it's math-related) and how to cope with those statistical anomalies we call "bad beats."

Chapter 16 – Losing Because You Don't Use Game Selection. You've probably heard someone say, at one point in their poker career, "I'm stuck two racks, but I can't leave—*it's a great game!*" Is it really? We explain why game selection is important, as well as how to differentiate a good game from one you should pass up.

Chapter 17 – Losing Because You've Forgotten The Goal of Poker.   Why do you play poker? Do you really, honestly know? Losing sight of the reason you're playing is often the biggest detriment to some players. We try to refresh your memory and help you focus on the goal at hand.

Chapter 18 – Twenty Hands at the Card Room. Our ten friends gather to battle it out against each other in an awesome spectacle of poker action. Who will prevail in this battle of might, wit, and downright confusion? You'll have to read on to find out.

Just have fun!

We must admit to one more motive for writing this book. We wanted to have fun while teaching others how to play better poker. And we did just that. Writing a book is never easy, and this book was no exception. But we did have a lot of good times and laughs along the way. We sincerely hope that we've conveyed that through our writing, and we'd love to hear that you've had just as good a time reading this book as we did in writing it.

This book will not turn you into a winning player overnight. However, by studying it you should be able to see many of the tactical, mathematical and psychological mistakes that you're making while playing poker. These are the primary reasons why you're losing at the tables. And you may be unaware that you're making these simple mistakes. If you make fewer of these errors you will lose less *and* win more.

Cast of Characters

In most poker books, you'll find your opponents labeled as "your left hand opponent (LHO)," "your right hand opponent (RHO)," "the button," "the big blind," or something similar. Sometimes you'll hear that the opponent is "loose," or "weak-tight," or some other descriptive to try to give you a hint about the action you *should* take.

The real world is different. Players have personalities, and they usually play to a specific pattern. This book is character driven. The ten players listed below (who are used almost exclusively) are the characters that drive this book. They're typical of the players you will face either online or in a cardroom. Here's a brief description of what makes each one tick.

Aaron. Aaron is a solid limit hold'em player. He's usually tight and aggressive, and is a big winner in his cardroom's low-limit games. However, he is just learning how to play no-limit hold'em.

Chris. Chris is a new player, and he considers himself to be the unluckiest player in the world. Chris *thinks* he knows what he is doing, but you might think otherwise. In fact, you *should* think otherwise.

Jerrod. Jerrod plays tight poker, so tight, in fact, that his friends have accused him of squeaking when he throws chips into the pot. He's recently taken up no-limit hold'em because he likes the fact that he can make big money when he gets big pairs.

Joan. Joan loves no-limit hold'em, where she can say her two favorite words, "All in." She's loose and aggressive, but not a complete maniac at the table as she's *slightly* cautious post-flop. She rarely "breaks even," as her wins tend to be big; however, so are her losses.

Justin. Justin learned the game on the Internet, and has only recently started to play live poker. He finds the game slow in the cardroom, and can get bored waiting for hands to play out. When he's bored, he'll liven up the game. He always wears mirrored sunglasses, a baseball cap, and a sweatshirt from his college.

Michelle. While Jerrod plays tight, Michelle plays loose. She loves to see flops, because any two cards can win. If the pot's unraised, it's a rare hand that she'll fold.

Mick. While Joan tends towards playing like a maniac, Mick *is* a maniac. Almost any two cards will do. He loves to raise with nothing, in limit or no-limit.

Mrs. Goldman. Mrs. Goldman tries to play well. Her husband has paid for lessons with a world-class tutor. Unfortunately, the saying "a little knowledge is a dangerous thing" can be applied to her actions at the card table. She accurately remembers bits and pieces of what her tutor has told her.

Nolan. Nolan plays like a professional. He can play almost any style of game, and is, in general, a tight/aggressive player. Normally, you'll find Nolan in a mid-limit or high-limit game (where he's often a winner).

Peter. Peter is a relatively new player, and tends to play a weak/tight brand of poker. When he's in over his head he'll play like a nit. He rarely wins a lot, nor does he lose a lot. His bluffs are few and far between.

Play Topics

The Money You Lose Playing Too Many Hands

Playing too loose is arguably the most common error in poker, and the one that will cost you the most money. It is also the first step in "the theory of compounding errors." For example, often times a player will limp in with a very speculative hand, such as J9s in middle position. It's not a particularly good hand, and should usually be folded in most situations. The player decides he'll take a look at the flop, and unless he flops a big hand, he will fold.

Even in theory, this strategy is a poor one. How often will our player flop a huge hand with J9s? Not often. And further, it's a hand that can catch good on the flop and be completely dominated (by a larger flush or straight, a Jack with a better kicker, etc.). Our player has what he thinks is enough to continue with the hand, so he does. And when he loses the hand on the river, his initial decision has cost him several big bets on a hand that he shouldn't have played at all. He has compounded his error.

Yeah, yeah, yeah. We know. You've heard it a million times. Everyone tells you that you're playing too loose and that you need to tighten up. But what does that really mean? And how do you do it?

Of the 169 possible starting hands you can be dealt in hold'em, how do you know which ones to play and when? Since this book is not specifically about hold'em, we're not going to attempt to answer this question. You won't find starting hand charts for any game in this book. Instead, we're going to be a bit more theoretical in our discussions. When it comes down to it, *almost* any hand is playable *if the circumstances are correct*. And this is where our conversation will begin—with a discussion of correct circumstances.

Starting hand charts are not specifically made for memorization. They are included in most books as a guideline. Learning the hand charts will guide you to your own style after you've mastered the basics. Discipline is an integral part of any serious player's game, and learning starting hand categories is one way to make sure you maintain that discipline. As you become comfortable with your game and develop your own personal style, you will find yourself making your own adjustments to these charts. But for now, let's consider this learning of hand charts a sort of basic training.

Cold Calling Errors

One of the biggest mistakes in the category of playing too many hands is cold-calling raises with hands that should be folded. Let's start with some examples to better illustrate this error.

Michelle is playing limit hold'em, sitting in middle position with K♥T♥. Normally, she might want to play a hand like this in late position in an unraised pot. In fact, Lou Krieger recommends you play this hand even in early position.[1] But in this particular hand there is a raise from the player *under the gun* (first to act after the blinds). This generally means a powerful hand, such as a big pair like AA-JJ or something like A♦K♦ or A♣Q♣. All of these hands are way ahead of Michelle's suited king. What kind of flop is she hoping for (aside from flopping a big straight or flush)? She really doesn't want to flop a king since she won't know if she's ahead or behind. And if a ten flops, she might have top pair with a good kicker and still be well behind an overpair. In this case, Michelle's K♥T♥ should be folded immediately.

Nolan is playing seven card stud. A 3 has brought it in and Nolan looks at his starting cards to find (J♥9♣) J♣, a nice raising hand. However, Chris, showing the K♣, has raised ahead of him, and Michelle with the Q♣ as her *door card* (the first up-card in seven card stud) has called the raise. What does Nolan think of his pair of jacks now? Not only is he possibly facing two hands that are likely beating the jacks, but any hope he had of a straight or flush is now greatly diminished with the K♣ and Q♣ already out. Nolan correctly folds.

---

[1]You'll find a starting hand chart in the book *Hold'em Excellence: From Beginner to Winner* on pages 39-40.

OK, one more example.

Jerrod is on the button in limit hold'em with 9♠8♠. After folding for almost forty minutes, this hand looks like gold. The first three players fold, and Peter (a tight, usually passive player) raises. This is the first hand Jerrod has seen this player play in a long time, and he immediately puts him on a quality holding. Most tight players are only raising with solid values (with an occasional bluff based on reputation), and this is a player you're not crazy about playing against. Everyone else folds. As Jerrod knows from his beginning hold'em book, 9♠8♠ is a drawing hand best played against multiple opponents. He certainly has *position* in this hand (he gets to act after Peter on every betting round), but with only one player against him (and *maybe* one or both of the blinds), he can't play this hand. Calling would be a big mistake.

The point is that hands you might normally play or even raise with can be rendered unplayable when facing a raise by a player acting before you. Every hand in poker is situational, and you need to pay careful attention to the action that has occurred before you act, as well as the action that might occur after.

Chasing Draws

Another common error is *chasing draws* (calling one or several bets in an attempt to make a straight or flush) when you shouldn't. You will often hear players bemoan their fate when an opponent catches a card to fill an inside straight draw (commonly referred to as a *gutshot*). The old poker adage, "never draw to an inside straight" is often correct. However, the saying should be edited to read, "never draw to an inside straight without the proper pot odds." If you're getting better than about 10 to 1 on the flop and you've got a gutshot draw, you can call the bet. If you've got overcards to the board, and there are three suits on the flop, you can even call a bet getting about 8 to 1. But anything less than that, you should fold. Let's look at an example.

Michelle is a loose player and often chases any kind of draw she flops. On this hand, she's holding 8♦3♦ in the *cutoff seat* (the seat to the immediate right of the button). Justin, an aggressive player in early position, put in his usual pre-flop raise. After Peter called from middle position, Michelle decided that since her cards were suited, she could also call the two bets cold. Everyone else in the hand folded, and three players saw a flop of 9♣J♣Q♥. Justin seemed to like this flop and bet out. Peter folded and the action was to Michelle. There were about eight bets in the pot (minus the rake). Michelle reasoned that she needed only one card, a ten, to be a winner. She happily called. This was a mistake, of course, as she was getting less than 8 to 1 pot odds on her call. Also notice that not only did she have just a gutshot, it was to the bottom end of the straight. If her magic ten did happen to fall, any king would beat her. Even worse, there were no diamonds on the board to give her a flush *re-draw* (an additional, unexpected draw that adds some value to a hand). In fact, the two clubs on the flop made the board even more dangerous.

The turn brought Michelle the card she thought she was looking for, the T♣. When Justin bet out, she immediately raised with her baby straight. When Justin only called, she knew her hand was good. She continued her thinking when the apparently harmless looking 4♣ came on the river. Even though Justin bet out a second time, Michelle assumed he was trying to bully her out of "her" pot, and she again raised him. Justin re-raised and Michelle re-raised him right back. With a perplexed look on his face, Justin sighed and called, flipping over K♣K♥ for the second-nut flush. Michelle smiled and turned over her little straight, not even noticing that Justin had finished with the better hand. The look on Michelle's face was one of surprise and sadness when she saw the huge pot being pushed to Justin. Had Michelle folded before the flop, she would have saved the fifteen small bets that were now in Justin's growing stack of chips.

It isn't always long-shot draws that get a player into trouble. Even common flush and straight draws can cost you a lot of bets if you chase without proper odds. Drawing hands are best played against multiple opponents, while high-card and big-pair hands are best played against fewer opponents. The reason is that the pots tend to be larger in multi-handed pots, and this gives you great odds for your drawing hands. In short, you don't need to win as often to show a profit. Still, you need to be careful with your drawing hands even when it looks like you'll be getting the correct odds. We explore this in the next two examples.

Chris considers himself a solid player. He's tight before the flop and he's aggressive when he has a hand. But Chris doesn't realize he has one major leak in his game: he chases draws too often. In this particular hand, Chris has J♣T♣ in early position. He decides not to scare any players away with a raise, so he just calls the big blind. Unfortunately, everyone else in the hand folds, including the small blind. There are now just two small bets in the pot. When the flop comes Q♣4♥7♣, Chris's eyes light up. He's flopped a flush draw. And when Nolan, the big blind, bets on the flop, Chris happily calls. After all, he's getting almost 3 to 1 on his call (three small bets minus the rake), and he's a 1.9 to 1 shot to make his flush by the river. But this is where he makes his mistake.

When the A♦ comes on the turn, Chris fails to make his flush. Nolan still seems to like his hand when he continues to bet. Now the pot contains a little less than three big bets (six small bets minus the rake). Determined to make his flush, Chris calls the bet with his 3 to 1 pot odds. But things have changed. With only one card to come, Chris is now a 4.2 to 1 underdog to make his flush on the last card. And facing two overcards, this call is very dangerous indeed. He's not getting the correct odds on his call, and as we'll soon see, there are still several cards that could trap him.

The J♥ comes on the river, and when Nolan bets for the third time, Chris looks at the five big bets in the pot and decides to make a *crying call* (a call on the last card that has little chance of success) with his third pair. He's not even surprised when Nolan turns over A♥7♦ and takes down the pot with two pair.

Chris's mistake was made in not considering the true odds of making his draw. When drawing to hands like straights and flushes, you must look at the entire hand and not just the hand at the moment. Had Chris looked ahead, he might have realized that if he missed his draw on the flop, his odds would be too poor to continue his draw on the turn. With this information, he would have made the correct move on the flop and folded. As it turned out, he lost three big bets by chasing a draw without proper pot odds.

In this next example, Chris finds himself in a wild and crazy hold'em game. The game has been going on all night, and with players like Mick in the game, it is rare to see the flop without at least a raise or two. So when Chris is on the button holding A♦8♦ and the pot hasn't been raised, he gladly limps in after two other players (Jerrod, a tight player, and Mick the maniac) and hopes the blinds decide to take it easy. It's Chris' lucky hand. Not only does the small blind fold, but the big blind decides to check. Four players see a flop of Q♦3♦3♠. Chris has flopped a flush draw, and he mentally starts to figure out just how big this pot is going to get and how much fun it will be to stack all of those chips. Michelle, the loose player in the big blind, decides to bet right out. *No problem*, Chris thinks. *After Jerrod and Mick call here, I'll be getting 7 to 1 on my nut flush draw. I might even raise.* But now Jerrod raises. To make matters worse, Mick re-raises. When the action gets to Chris, there are ten small bets in the pot, but Chris has to put three bets in, so his odds have been reduced from 7 to 1 down to about 3 to 1 when the rake is factored in. Further, Jerrod might re-raise when it gets back to him. Still, the prospect of a huge pot is enticing, so Chris calls.

Looking disgusted, Michelle decides to abandon her hand. And sure enough, Jerrod now re-raises and Mick calls. Chris is getting 16 to 1 on this call, and although he's pretty wary of the action in front of him, he calls. Taking the rake away, the pot now contains about eight big bets. On the turn, the A♠ falls, and when Jerrod bets, Mick suddenly gets aggressive again and puts in the raise. Facing 11 to 2 odds, Chris is still getting the correct price to draw to his flush. However, the board is not pretty. After heavy action on the paired flop, the hand has become even more aggressive when another overcard hits the turn and puts a second flush draw on the board. Chris should now realize that even if he makes the call, he'll still be facing two more big bets on this round in all likelihood, and even though he's getting just enough odds to call for a flush, he's probably not going to win the pot even if he makes his flush. He correctly folds.

As the hand played out, Jerrod and Mick went to four bets on the turn and two more bets each on the river when the Q♥ hit. Mick took the pot with K♦Q♠ (a full house) beating Jerrod's 4♣3♥ (trip threes). Note that Chris would have lost even more bets on the turn had he chased with his flush draw.

Chasing with Poor Holdings

How many times have you raised before the flop with a hand like A♥K♣, had five people call your raise, and then completely missed the flop? It's bet and raised before it gets to you. How much do you like your Big Slick now?

Sometimes even the best laid plans go wrong. Winning poker players know how to adjust to these situations, accepting a small loss and moving on to the next hand. Unfortunately for most, it's not that simple. In your poker career, you will undoubtedly see player after player who just can't let go of a hand even when it's obvious that his hand can't win. Knowing when to lay down a hand is such an important part of winning poker that if you take nothing else from this chapter but this one small section, the price you paid for this book will have been well worth it.

We all love to see great starting hands, especially big pairs. But your hand is defined on the flop, not before it, and if you've completely missed the flop, it's time to start looking for reasons to fold. Here are some typical examples.

Our new player Chris finds himself in late position with T♣T♠. After two limpers, Chris feels justified in calling along with his pair, hoping to hit a set on the flop. One player calls behind Chris, but Justin (the aggressive player from a previous example) raises from the button. Everyone calls the raise after the blinds fold, and they see the flop four-handed. The flop is A♥Q♦8♥. Everyone checks to Justin who bets (of course). One of the early limpers is Nolan, a very solid player who most regulars believe might be a pro. Nolan raises (after checking). The other limper folds, but Chris looks down at his two tens and just can't let them go. He calls the two bets cold. After Justin calls the raise, Nolan comes out betting on the turn when it comes K♦. For some unknown reason, Chris calls. Justin calls as well. The river is the 3♦, and Nolan immediately bets again. Chris has missed his set and now feels that he has to call because the pot is so big. He calls, and much to his chagrin, Justin now raises. Nolan calls with a disgusted look on his face, and Chris follows suit. Nolan turns up A♣Q♣ for the flopped two pair, and before Chris even mucks, Justin turns over 8♦7♦ for the runner-runner flush.

If you're asking yourself, *"Why on earth was Chris calling all that way with nothing but a pair of tens,"* then you probably have a good handle on when to lay down a hand (but read on anyway). It seems nuts, but many, many players will call to the river with nothing but a medium pocket pair (or worse, unimproved hands like AK). It's a horrible error most of the time, as can be evidenced from Chris's hand. It is rare to have the proper odds to chase the set, and usually when those odds are actually present, even hitting the set won't be enough to win the hand. Don't fall into this trap. When you're holding a pair and the action is heavy on a scary flop (overcards and straight and flush draws), just fold.

Not convinced? OK, here's another typical hand.

After the frustration with the pair of tens, Chris is happy to find A♥K♥ on the very next hand. So, after one player limps, he raises. The big blind and the original limper call the raise. The flop comes T♣8♦7♠ and Justin bets from the big blind. Although he is just a player with "the look" (ball cap, sunglasses, Internet poker t-shirt), he seems to have at least some idea of how to play. The limper folds, and Chris calls. Why? The board is connected with action before him, and he has nothing but overcards. Even if one hits, is it good? Calling in this spot is a mistake.

The turn brings the 6♠, and after Justin again bets, Chris calls once more. The river is the A♣ and Justin bets for the third time. Chris thinks of raising, but decides to just call. It's his only smart move after the flop. Justin flips up 9♦4♠ for the straight, and Chris doesn't even show his one-pair loser.

Chasing to the river with just overcards and no draws at all is a losing proposition. As Chris found out, even if you hit your hand, you can still lose. Chris called with nothing, caught a little something on the river to stay in, and ended up losing seven small bets on the hand (as opposed to just two had he folded on the flop) because he couldn't let it go.

Many players will call to the river with two big cards or even nothing more than a bare ace (no connecting or suited cards with it) hoping to catch something to win the hand. Little do they know, the old "one-pair draw" is one of the quickest ways to the ATM. Don't make this mistake. Even if you've raised before the flop, if you completely miss the flop and there's been action before you, it's almost always best to fold and wait for the next hand.

Playing Too Few Hands

Although it may seem counterintuitive, it is very possible to play *too* tight. New players who have been playing for a while and playing way too many hands will almost always fall into a common trap. The scenario usually starts with a new player who really enjoys the game but seems to lose more than he wins. So he buys a book or two and begins his life-long study of the game. After a few weeks of absorbing information and discovering that he's been playing way too many hands, he decides to tighten up. But what he ends up doing is over-compensating for his errors and instead of playing speculative hands and taking the number of opponents and pot odds into consideration, he folds nearly everything but aces or kings.

He *thinks* he's practicing discipline and playing smart poker, but what he's really doing is costing himself lots of money by not getting involved in hands he is justified in playing. What started out to be a correction of multiple bad habits has turned into the creation of new ones to replace the old.

Playing tight and selective is paramount to winning poker, but don't over-use the concept. It's fine to play draws and even cold-call pre-flop raises with hands like 9♥9♣. Don't limit yourself to playing nothing other than AA, KK, QQ and AKs. It's another sure path to the rail.

The Money You Lose By Not Taking The Initiative

Peter is a winning player—barely. He is very tight and he only plays quality hands. Peter usually breaks even in a session, or comes out slightly ahead. Every so often he loses while holding big starting cards. He'll occasionally lament on how many times players draw out on him and hit their hands.

Peter is a typical player. He is in what some people might call *stage two* of his poker development. He's learned that tight play is a great way to save a lot of money. But what he doesn't realize is that it is possible to play *too* tight and *too* cautious.

Let's see where Peter might be going wrong. He's on the button holding K♥K♦ in a $5-$10 limit hold'em game. After three limpers, Mick raises from the cutoff seat. Peter knows there is no way he can fold kings in this spot, and he is aware that Mick plays too many hands and usually plays them aggressively. So he puts $10 into the pot and thinks, *No you don't. Not this time!* After the blinds and one limper fold, the remaining two limpers call the extra $5 as well, and they go to the flop four-handed. There is $52 in the pot (we'll ignore the rake in this example).

The flop is almost perfect for Peter: K♣3♠9♦. The two limpers check, and as expected, Mick bets the $5. Even cautious Peter knows that top set is a great hand, so he raises to $10. The two limpers fold and Mick makes it three-bets. Peter calls the extra $5. There is now $82 in the pot.

The turn card is the 7♠. Mick fires out another bet. Peter still thinks he has the best hand (as any player holding the absolute nuts should know) so he calls the $10. Heading to the river, the pot is $102.

The river is the 6♠. Mick bets again and Peter calls with conviction, expecting to take the $122 pot. But when Mick turns over A♠4♠ for the nut flush, Peter's smile diminishes as the chips are pushed toward Mick's growing stack. Peter laments his fate quietly to himself and waits for the next hand.

So where did Peter go wrong? This is a common scenario. Players who lack aggression will often lose a nice pot to an apparent bad beat, when what they've actually done is given an opponent an opportunity to win. Peter had the second best starting hand before the flop. A maniac raised (as he usually did), and there is no reason at all why Peter shouldn't have re-raised with his kings. That was his first mistake. He probably could have thinned the field right there, but instead he allowed other players to get into the pot cheaply, thus giving Mick the correct odds for his bets and raises.

Peter's second mistake was on the flop. *But wait, didn't he raise on the flop?* Yes, but when he was re-raised, he just called. Peter had the best possible hand on the flop, and against an overly aggressive player like Mick, he should have made it four bets instead of passively calling.

On the turn, Peter again played like a wimp. Mick bet into him, and although he still had the very best possible hand, he only called. There were about ten big bets in the pot and Mick was about a 4 to 1 underdog to make his flush. He had excellent odds for his bet here, but only because Peter didn't act strongly enough with his set. Had Peter played the hand a little more aggressively, Mick would not have been in the position to take down this big pot.

Peter thinks he lost this hand due to bad luck, but it was bad play that cost him the pot, not the cards. Had he played the hand aggressively, he would have most likely chased Mick out and won a decent pot. Instead, he played passively and lost a pot that should have been his. Even after chasing some players from the pot, Peter might have won a similar-sized pot once Mick folded.

Sit down in any $3-$6 hold'em game in Las Vegas. You will usually see six to eight people seeing every flop (see Chapter 2, *The Money You Lose Playing Too Many Hands*, beginning on page 11), and very seldom do you see a pre-flop raise.[2] You will also see most players just calling down bets. They might have nothing, or they might have a huge hand, but most of them are afraid to put more money in the pot even when doing so would give them a better chance to win.

Peter is a typical player in these games. Although he plays much tighter than most, he is afraid to bet or raise when he should. This costs Peter money—*a lot* of money.

Playing scared is a term you might have heard before. It simply means playing a tight, ultra-conservative game and not taking even the slightest of calculated risks by way of aggression. Countless times we've seen players limp with aces (not to make a move, but just because they were afraid to raise), kings, queens, ace-king— you get the idea. When you're not raising or re-raising pre-flop with your premium hands, you're giving up a tremendous edge. Sure, your tight play can save you many bets, but you also need to realize that the other side of the coin—*maximizing* your wins—is just as important as *minimizing* your losses. Further, aggressive play not only makes those winning hands more profitable, but it also allows you to win more hands.

Chris is a friend of Peter's. They actually learned poker together and have a similar style. But Chris likes to gamble more, so he plays more hands.

Chris related this hand to Peter and can't figure out what he did wrong. He's in middle position holding A♥K♣ in a $3-$6 hold'em game, and knowing he should be aggressive with hands like this, he raises. So far, so good. Only Michelle calls from the button. There is $15 in the pot ($1 of rake has been taken). The blinds fold, and they see a flop heads-up of 7♦Q♥3♠. Nothing scary at all, but as Chris notices with a grimace, he has completely missed the flop, so he checks. Michelle checks behind him. The turn card is the 2♦. Again, Chris has nothing and elects to check. Michelle checks as well. The river is a harmless looking 6♣. Chris decides to bet $6 and take the pot. Since Michelle has checked on the flop and on the turn, Chris reasons that she has nothing. To his surprise, Michelle has the audacity to raise! Curious to see what she has and also sus-

---

[2]It should be noted that in California, games of this limit and similar limits are usually very aggressive with many pre-flop raises. The games in Las Vegas tend to play much more passively due to a great deal of the players being tourists who are new to the game. This is in contrast with the usual players in California who play on a much more regular basis.

pecting her of bluffing, he calls. She turns over 6♦6♥ and wins the $37 pot with her rivered set.

"Geeze, I get rivered every time!" Chris complains. Not realizing that he was never ahead in the hand, Chris is also missing a very important point: he played the hand horribly.

Sure, his pre-flop raise was fine, but on a weak flop like the one that came up, he should have bet against his lone opponent. More often than not, the player who bets the flop will win the hand. Chris thought it best to check since he only held ace-high, but he was playing the cards, not the situation. He needed to take the initiative and bet. And when Michelle checked behind him on the flop, he should have bet the turn when another rag came off the deck. However, he reasoned that since he had nothing, he was better off saving a bet. Do notice that a bet by Chris any time before the river would have earned him the $16 pot.

Chris' bet on the river was fine. After Michelle had two opportunities to bet, she checked, so he naturally reasoned that she had nothing. His call on the river, however, is debatable. Sure, Michelle could have been bluffing, but probably not. And with only five big bets in the pot on the river, Chris has to be sure that Michelle will bluff at least one time in five hands in this situation to make the call. Knowing she's a loose but straightforward player, Chris probably should have folded his ace-high here. But like most new players, Chris is always suspicious of the bluff.

The main mistake Chris made was not betting on the flop. Remember that most of the time, the flop isn't going to help you. And in that same vein, *it is not going to help your lone opponent either.* There was only one card in the playing zone,[3] and with no straight or flush draws, there was no present danger. Chris' failure to bet this non-threatening flop cost him a chance to win the pot. Remember, Michelle had an underpair to the board. Many players will still call all bets to the river when they hold any pocket pair, but Michelle had been a little less of a gambler than that during the course of the game, and Chris noted that he rarely saw Michelle take down big pots even though she seemed to see nearly every flop.

---

[3]The set of cards containing 9, T, J, Q, K and A are commonly referred to as cards in the "playing zone."

Let's take a look at a more complex example. This situation takes place in every game that has at least one aggressive player in it. By aggressive, we mean a player who always seems to be raising before the flop and betting on and beyond the flop. This player has either amassed a large stack of chips or a large stack of ATM slips. He's almost never "about even" during a session. He's an action player, and he's usually playing too many hands and over-playing the hands he gets. He loves a loose, passive table because he can steamroll his way to a nice profit. He doesn't play scared, although he does play foolishly in many circumstances. Overall, this type of player is a big lifetime loser at poker, but there's no telling the huge amount of chips he can stack up if the cards fall his way. Joan is one such player.

Peter finds himself in a $5-$10 limit hold'em game with the beautiful but deadly Joan. She has been playing her usual aggressive, ram'em, jam'em style and has been running over the table. After nearly four hours of play, this devil in disguise has more than tripled her buy-in and there seems to be no stopping her. The whole table is afraid to play pots with her. She seems to bet every flop if checked to her as if she's hit every one. She also raises most flops if there is a bet in front of her, and more often than not, she takes the pots uncontested before the showdown. The air is thick with frustration.

In one particular hand, Peter is in late position with A♦T♥. There have been three limpers before him, including Joan. It's been a very loose, passive game (except for Joan), and Peter knows that in this type of game, A♦T♥ is a very playable hand from late position, so he calls as well. Both blinds call, and after $3 in rake is taken, there is $27 in the pot. The flop looks great to Peter when it comes 9♣A♥3♦. Everyone checks to Joan, who throws in a $5 bet as expected. Peter just calls with his top pair, and everyone else folds, not wanting to tangle with the dreaded Joan. The pot is now $37. The turn is the 6♥ and again, Joan bets. Peter simply calls the $10, bringing the pot to $57. The river is the. 4♦ Joan again bets, and Peter simply calls. Nothing on the boards is threatening, but Peter just doesn't want to mess with Joan for fear of being raised or re-raised out of this massive $77 pot. Joan grins sweetly and turns over 4♣3♣ for the winning two-pair. Where did Peter go wrong?

If you said "on the flop," you're correct. Peter should have raised the flop. Sometimes a raise for information is a good tactic when you have a good hand that is not the nuts. Joan might have called the raise, but she might also have checked and folded on the turn had Peter bet again. Peter could have won the pot had he taken the initiative and bet the flop with his top pair, but instead, he allowed himself to be bullied and, in doing so, he allowed his opponent to make her hand.

When facing an aggressive opponent, you need to make a stand with your better hands (and sometimes even with hands that might not rate to be the best at the moment). Against passive players, the bully will continue to play her game as long as no one is playing back at her. You need to force the bully into decisions she is not used to making, and put her on the defensive. Once you throw your opponent off balance even a little bit, you'll begin to expose her weaknesses. And once you do that, those big pots will be much more easily attainable.

Sometimes you have to take the concept a step further. Sometimes raising or even check-raising with hands as weak as second pair will be just what you need to throw off your tougher opponents. But make sure you're making plays like this against players who are actually paying attention and who will most likely adjust to them. In the small-stakes games, tight, aggressive and straightforward play will earn you the chips.

A number of years ago, a new phrase was coined in the poker world: Fancy Play Syndrome (FPS). Many new or intermediate players, learning plays like raising and check-raising with second pair or with a draw, will often take it to an extreme. They get caught up in the fun of making these plays, not realizing that they probably lose money in the long run because their opponents have finally caught on. These players suffer from FPS, and the results can be devastating to their bankrolls. Keep these special plays in your poker arsenal, but don't use them to excess.

One last concept on the topic of taking the initiative may very well be the most important. Poker, as no doubt you've already been told, is a game of incomplete information. You (as well your opponents) must make countless decisions in every poker session based on very little information. You watch your opponents, their betting patterns in all situations, look for tells, talk to them, etc. Every little bit of data plugged into the poker computer of your brain assists you in analyzing the situation for a more accurate and appropriate play for each individual situation. But what if this information is flawed in some way? What if, after playing twenty sessions with Nolan and getting an excellent read on his style of play, he check-raises you with a flush draw one afternoon and you end up laying down the best hand, knowing that Nolan *never* semi-bluffs with his draws? Never is a pretty strong word, especially in the world of poker. And apparently Nolan knows this, and has exploited the concept to your detriment.

But it gets worse. The next time you play with Nolan and the flop brings a flush draw, Nolan check-raises you. Suddenly, images of a past session come back to you. You think *ah, I know what he's doing. He's semi-bluffing a flush draw again. Not this time, pal.* You re-raise him with your top pair, but Nolan just comes right back and pops it again. This gives you pause, of course, because Nolan isn't the most aggressive player you've ever faced, and he usually only plays his big hands in this fashion. So you just call him down, and when he shows you that he flopped top set, you're left wondering just what kind of player Nolan really is. You thought you knew, but apparently things have changed. Either that, or your initial perceptions were inaccurate.

Do you see what has happened here? Nolan has mixed up his play against you, and he's now keeping you guessing. Nolan realizes that the less predictable he is, the harder he'll be to read, and ultimately, the tougher an opponent he will become.

What lesson do you learn from this? It's simple. Don't play the same way in every situation every time. Change your play, and change it as much as *effectively* possible. Don't always check-raise with a flopped set. Just come right out betting sometimes, like you might do with a flush draw or second pair, or even top pair. If you've raised pre-flop and you end up flopping a big hand, don't always bet out just because you raised pre-flop. And if you've raised pre-flop and completely missed, don't just bet anyway. Check and fold some of the time, and check-raise other times (against the more aggressive players, of course). What you're doing isn't quite randomizing your play, but it is giving you enough room to change it up and confuse your opponents. The more you confuse them, the more mistakes they will make. At the end of the year, that translates to more money in your pocket.

How many times have you asked an experienced player for advice on a particular hand, situation or player, only to hear "It depends..." that dreaded, cover-all reply? Your experienced friends aren't using "it depends" as an escape hatch. Each situation really does depend on a myriad of circumstances, each one affecting the proper decision and outcome. Don't get stuck in the rut of using your "pet play" all the time, because pretty soon, no one will fall for your little tricks, and countermeasures will be taken to extract your money from your wallet. *Keep them guessing!*

Using aggression and taking the initiative are two very important weapons. We believe that the lack of aggression is ranked only behind poor starting hand selection in the ordered list of mistakes people make in poker. By not being aggressive and not taking the initiative, you will allow players to catch up and beat you when the board is threatening, you will allow yourself to be intimidated, and you will become too predictable.

Many people think of poker as a war, but here's another analogy to ponder: Poker is like that game we all played as kids, Capture the Flag. Think of your opponents' chips as the opposing team's flag. It's right before your eyes and ready for the taking. But if you sit back and simply react to the attacks of your opponents, you'll never get it. Sure, your opponents will never get your flag because of your disciplined, cautionary defense. But *you* will never win the game.

Favor action over reaction. Make a stand. Go for the throat when you sense weakness and uncertainty in your opponent. Attack when you feel the time is right. Don't rely on simple defense to win the war for you. Your offense is just as important, and you must use it. Over time, you'll discover that the more you take the initiative, the easier and more natural it becomes. And when you begin to notice weak play in others, you will finally be there. If you catch yourself saying things like *man, how could he have not raised there,* then you're well on your way.

The Money You Lose By Not Recognizing You Are Beat

"**H**ey, did you hear about the wedding?" Nolan asked Jerrod as they took a break from a great $3-$6 hold'em game.

"What wedding?"

"Chris is getting married. Didn't you hear?"

"No, I had no idea! That's great news. Who's the bride?"

Nolan grinned. "A pair of kings!" Nolan then burst into a fit of laughter as Jerrod groaned at the bad joke.

But was it really a joke?

We've all heard the phrase, "Don't get married to your hand." This usually refers to big pairs or Big Slick, but it can also mean a decent hand that flops good but faces considerable action from another opponent. The meaning is, of course, to recognize when your hand is no longer the best hand, no matter how good it might have looked before the flop.

Nolan was right about Chris. You might remember from a previous chapter that Chris likes to call way too much, even when it is apparent that his hand is not the best. Chris plays tight enough, but he just can't seem to let go of some hands. And this is especially true with his big pairs.

Nolan's comment was brought on by a $3-$6 hand played just before they decided to take a break. Chris was in late position with K♠K♣. Michelle and Peter limped in, and Mick, as he had done so many times, raised in late-middle position. Chris knew enough to re-raise with his kings, and he was able to eliminate one of the limpers as Peter folded. Only Michelle and Mick called, making Chris sure neither opponent had the dreaded aces. The three players went to the flop for $9 each. Counting the limper and the blinds, there was $35 in the pot (minus the rake).

The flop looked pretty good to Chris: Q♥9♥J♦. He had an overpair and a gutshot straight draw. Michelle checked, and maniacal Mick fired $3 into the pot. Chris raised to $6 with his big pair, and after Michelle called the $6 cold, Mick raised again, making the bet $9. Chris was aware of Mick's aggressive tendencies. He'd seen Mick bet and raise to the river with nothing but a bare king on a prior hand. He *knew* he was ahead in this hand, but he didn't want to scare Michelle out or tip Mick off to his big hand, so he just called the extra $3, waiting to spring the trap on the turn. Michelle called as well, and they went to the turn with $62 (minus the rake) in the pot.

The next card off the deck was the 8♦. Michelle checked, and as expected, Mick bet $6. Chris decided to finally reveal the true strength of his hand and cut out three neat stacks of four $1 chips; a raise to $12. Michelle called the two bets yet again, muttering something about the pot being too big to fold. But Mick again raised, making the bet $18. Not to be bluffed out by the maniac (Chris secretly despised Mick anyway), Chris re-raised to $24. With a hopeless look on her face, Michelle called another $12, and didn't even flinch when Mick capped the betting at $30.[4] Had this been a heads-up pot, Chris would have raised again, but since Michelle was still in the hand, he was not permitted to do so, and he called the last $6 as did Michelle. Having each put in $30 on the turn, the pot had swelled to $152 (minus the rake), a *huge* pot for a $3/$6 game.

The river card was the K♥, giving Chris top set. He smiled, knowing he was surely good now. But Michelle, sitting a little straighter in her chair, came out suddenly with a bet of $6. Mick raised to $12, and Chris, not realizing that there was almost certainly a straight out against *him*, made it $18 to go. Michelle raised again, making

---

[4]In Las Vegas, the standard rule in multi-way pots is one bet and four raises. In other places such as California, the rule is a bet and three raises. Throughout this book, we use both rules since some of you will be playing in Las Vegas, and others will be playing in California, online, or other places where the second rule is in effect.

it $24, and Mick, not realizing that there was also a possible flush out against *him*, again capped the betting at $30. Mick called the remaining bets, as did Michelle, of course. After all, she had the winning hand with A♥4♥. Mick threw down his cards in disgust, T♦8♣. He had actually flopped a straight and rivered a larger one. Chris slowly flipped up his two kings, dumbfounded that he had the third best hand. He sat there shocked as Michelle dragged the pot that totaled over $240—the largest pot Chris had ever seen, and a pot *he* was planning on adding to his now decimated stack of chips.

Nolan and Jerrod got up from the table for their break, both shaking their heads in amazement. Nolan was a smart player and knew that Chris was beaten. But why didn't Chris see it? Too often, after folding for what seems like hour after hour, a big pair like kings or queens seems like a gift from the poker gods, a sure sign that *finally* some chips are coming your way. You raise (as well you should), but when the betting and raising starts to indicate that your kings may no longer be good, you often fail to recognize the warning signs. You end up pushing too hard with a hand that, while it may have been best before the flop or on the flop, is now second best (or worse).

Frustration can cause us to do things we know are wrong (at least, we know they're wrong when we are thinking clearly). Our emotions alter our perception—even if only temporarily—and cause us to play hands in an over-aggressive manner when it should be obvious that we are no longer in contention to win the pot. No matter how good a hand looks before the flop, we need to be very much aware of the action and the texture of the board (in flop games). Part of this is taking the other players into consideration (see Chapter 5, *The Money You Lose Not Taking the Other Players Into Consideration*, beginning on page 38). When the tightest player at the table makes it three bets to you on the flop and your aces have not improved, you need to start thinking about the hands you might be facing.

Big pairs can be beaten. Although AA is the best hand before the flop, you might be surprised by some facts. Here are some numbers[5] for you to ponder:

Your Hand	The Hand You Face	Your Chance of Winning
A♦A♣	K♠K♥	81.25%
A♦A♣	Q♠J♠	80.29%
A♦A♣	T♠9♠	77.23%

Against another pair, and even against decent suited connectors, aces are still a pretty big favorite. But watch what happens when you add one more hand to the mix.

Your Hand	The Hands You Face	Your Chance of Winning
A♦A♣	K♠K♥ and J♣J♥	66.45%
A♦A♣	K♠K♥ and T♠9♠	63.50%

Yes, you're still a solid favorite, but it's hard to imagine that aces are going to win all the time now, isn't it? Now let's have some fun and add another hand to the competition.

Your Hand	The Hands You Face	Your Chance of Winning
A♦A♣	K♠K♥, J♣J♥ and 8♦8♥	53.83%
A♦A♣	K♠K♥, 3♣3♥ and T♠9♠	50.05%

Against just three decent starting hands, you're barely a favorite to win the pot half the time. And just for kicks, let's see what one more hand does to your chances. We know that in the loose games that are so abundant these days, players aren't always playing the best starting hands, so we'll assume your fourth opponent plays two random cards.

Your Hand	The Hands You Face	Your Chance of Winning
A♦A♣	K♠K♥, J♣J♥, 8♦8♥ and 6♦4♣	42.83%
A♦A♣	K♠K♥, 3♣3♥, T♠9♠ and 6♦4♣	41.07%

---

[5]The calculations in this chapter were performed using Andrew Prock's *PokerStove*, available for free download at http://www.pokerstove.com.

How do you like your aces now?

Actually, you should still be fond of them. Even though you're no longer a favorite over *all* of the other hands, the pair of aces is still the hand that's most likely to win the pot. But don't get too attached to that big pair. As you can see, the more players you face, the less chance you have of winning the pot. The good news, however, is the fact that more players means a larger pot when you do win, so your expected value is about the same, and sometimes even higher (but don't tell that to the know-it-all who loves to tell the entire table how important it is to eliminate players when you have aces).

Perhaps a couple more examples will make the point a little clearer. Mick is a loose, aggressive player who loves to bully his opponents out of pots. Early in many sessions, he is successful. However, sometimes his more observant opponents will catch on that he doesn't always have "the goods" when he is betting or raising, and they will start to call him down with hands that usually wouldn't warrant a call. Such was the case when Joan got tangled up in a $1/$2 blinds no-limit hold'em pot she would later wish to forget.

It was the first hand of a new game, and each player had started with the mandatory $500 buy-in. Under the gun, Joan made her standard raise to $8. Nothing was out of the ordinary, except for the fact that Joan actually had a hand this time: A♠A♣. Michelle, a habitual calling station who often cold-called raises with poor holdings, found 9♥7♥ in front of her. Knowing the value of suited cards, Michelle decided she had an easy call. When the action got to Mick, one of our known maniacs, he made his usual re-raise to $25 holding a respectable K♦6♦ (well, respectable for Mick anyway). Everyone folded back around to Joan who decided to disguise her hand a little and just call. After all, she had the best two starting cards and she didn't want to scare anyone out of what was shaping up to be a pretty nice pot. After Joan called the $17 (recall she had already bet $8), Michelle called the additional $17 as well and they saw the flop 3-handed with a pot of about $75 after the rake.

The flop came K♥5♥A♥. Joan decided to slow-play her flopped top set (the three hearts on the board weren't going to scare her, not with the monster she was holding) and just checked. Michelle tried to conceal her own excitement and was fairly successful. She also checked, happy that she'd flopped a flush but very worried that someone might have a larger one. So Mick, seeing he had flopped second pair and seeing no aggression before him decided to bet out and take the pot right then. He fired $80 into the pot and waited for Joan to fold. But Joan, still content to slow-play her set of aces just called. Michelle called as well, not being able to fold even though she was practically convinced that someone had a bigger flush. There was $235 in the pot going to the turn.

Now it was Mick's turn to conceal his excitement. The 6♣ was dealt as the fourth board card, giving him two pair. Now he was certain he had the best hand. Joan, acting first, decided that the 6♣ wasn't a scary card and again checked. She loved to trap opponents for all of their chips, and this was an opportunity to trap *two* players. Besides, she reasoned that since Michelle wasn't betting, she must be on some kind of draw, and Mick the maniac was always bluffing, so who knows what he had. *Probably not much*, she thought. Yes, a check was safe here. So, she was surprised to see Michelle come out with a bet of $100 into the large pot. She was thinking about how much to raise her when she heard Mick suddenly chirp, "Raise!" He slid three stacks of red[6] into the center; a $200 raise of Michelle's bet (making it $300 for Joan to call).[7]

With her ears filled with the sound of old-time cash registers, Joan loudly declared, "All-in!" and shoved the rest of her stack into the pot. After Mick's raise to $300, this was only $95 more, and she was certain Mick would call her (unless he was on a complete bluff). To make things even more delightful, Michelle decided to make the call for all of her chips with her flush. She almost folded, still fearing that bigger flush, but decided she would gamble a little.

Mick quickly called his remaining $95, pushing the total pot to almost $1,500. Seeing that all the players were in, Mick turned over his cards and proudly proclaimed, "Top pair no good, kids! I've got *two!*"

---

[6]In most of the United States, red chips are worth $5 each. In most locations in California, *yellow* chips are worth $5 each. In this example, each stack of red is worth $100.

[7]The reader should be aware of the oddity of this raise. The bet of $300 left Mick with only $95 in chips. He was pot-committed, which meant he would most likely be forced to commit his last chips anyway due to pot odds. He would have been better off to just push it all-in here.

Not to be outdone by the arrogant Mick, Joan turned over her cards and said, "Yeah, but I've got *three*!" You can imagine the surprise on both faces when Michelle sheepishly turned over her two hearts for the flopped flush and said, "Oh, you mean I have the best hand? Wow! I thought I was beat for sure."

The river card did not pair the board, and Michelle raked in the monster pot. Mick reached into his front pocket and grabbed a large banded stack of bills for a re-buy (something his aggressive style had helped him grow accustomed to). Joan was too distraught to continue, however, and simply got up from her seat and walked out of the poker room. She felt sick.

Although the two examples we've covered so far are a little extreme, the point we're trying to make is that you need to be very aware of the betting action and the tendencies of the players performing such actions. Had Joan not become so infatuated with her aces, she would have realized that all that action on a one-suited flop most likely meant someone had a flush. Further, the action on the turn should have slammed it into her head that she was no longer holding the best hand.

Here are two things to remember all the time when playing any form of poker:

Look at the board (or boards if you're playing a stud game). Even if you have a really good starting hand, or even if you've flopped something great, look for reasons to fold. We're not telling you to make excuses to fold, but to just be aware of the possibility that you're in trouble. The best way to stay out of trouble is to recognize when it comes up. If the board is all suited, connected big cards, or perhaps one big card and a pair, the first warning bell should be ringing in your ears. With practice, this should become second nature. Recognizing when the board is scary and potentially threatening—even if you have a large piece of it—is a skill you need to master.

When the board is scary, pay very close attention to the betting action. If it is substantial, you've just heard your second warning bell. Unless you hold the nuts, the near nuts, or a draw to the nuts with adequate odds, you might want to strongly consider folding and wait for a better spot.

Monsters Under The Bed

As with any poker concept (especially the one you've just learned), this idea of cautious play can be taken too far—*way too far*. In fact, if you're too cautious, your good intentions can cost you a lot of money.

You remember Peter, right? He's our weak-tight player, trying to play tight like he's learned in his poker books and trying to avoid losing a lot of money. He thinks this is the best way to play, but what he doesn't realize is that being overly cautious is costing him a lot of money. Take this recent hand Peter played against some very aggressive players.

In a very loose and wild $8-$16 limit hold'em game at Bellagio over spring break, Peter was seated to the immediate left of Justin, one of the craziest gamblers at the table. Justin, you'll recall from a previous chapter, was a young kid with sunglasses, a baseball cap and an Internet poker room t-shirt. He was fast and aggressive, but also very loose and reckless. Peter tried to avoid playing against Justin when he could, but it was difficult because Justin was in almost every hand. To make things even more difficult, Mick was in the game too. Although Peter had played with Mick many times before and knew he was aggressive, he'd never seen Mick on this level before. He figured it was the influence of Justin being at the table. When two maniacs go to war, the game is usually very profitable, but the swings can be brutal.

Peter was in late position with Q♦Q♣. He knew this was a great hand, and when Mick raised in front of him and Justin called, he decided it would be a good spot to re-raise. It was uncharacteristic of Peter to do this, but he really was trying to step up to the next level and he knew he had to be more aggressive. Both Mick and Justin called the raise, and they saw the flop three-handed with $60 in the pot (before the rake, which we will ignore for this example) ($16 x 3, plus the $4 small blind and the $8 big blind).

The flop was perfect for Peter: Q♥9♥9♦. He had flopped a full house! And to his surprise, Mick came out with a bet. Justin called the $8 and Peter raised to $16. Mick called the additional $8 but Justin now raised to $24. This gave Peter pause. He knew Justin was loose and wild, but *he* had a *monster*. What could Justin have? Pocket nines? Peter raised again and Mick decided he'd had enough and folded. Justin came back with another raise. Peter was certain he was now up against quads, and he decided to just call. The pot was now $156 ($60, plus $16 from Mick plus $40 each from Justin and Peter).

The turn brought an offsuit 7, and Justin bet $16. Peter thought about trying a raise one more time, but decided that he didn't want to lose any more money than he had to on this hand. He couldn't fold, so he just called. There was now $188 in the pot.

The river was a harmless 3, and Justin bet out again. Peter, looking defeated, called the final $16 bet and nearly fell out of his chair when Justin turned over 9♣8♦ for nothing more than trips. The dealer pushed a shocked Peter the $220 pot.

Now a pot of almost fourteen big bets is certainly a nice win, but do you see where Peter went wrong? Peter flopped a monster, yet he feared an even bigger hand when a known maniac applied a little pressure. Peter didn't consider other possible hands that Justin could have been playing. Being as loose and aggressive as he is, Justin could have had A9, K9, Q9, J9, T9, 99 (a very slim chance, as you'll see in a moment), and even a hand as weak as 97. He could have also held AK, KQ or even KJ. A smaller pair was yet another possibility, or even a large pair like KK or JJ. He might have even had aces and just chosen a bad time to over-play them.

All of these hands were possible, but Peter feared the worst and decided to give Justin credit for flopping the quads. Perhaps Peter should have done a little research beforehand. If he had, he would have known that the odds of flopping quads (when holding a pocket pair) are 407 to 1![8] While this does happen from time to time, it is not something Peter needs to be overly concerned with, especially considering the nature of his opponent and the large number of possible hands his opponent might play in the same fashion.

---

[8]There are (50 x 49 x 48)/(3 x 2) = 19,600 possible flops. 1 x 1 x 48 = 48 of them will give you quads. Probability of flopping quads = 48/19,600 = 0.24%; Odds = (19,600/48) = 407.3:1. Note that if Peter takes his own two cards into account, the numbers change a bit. Now there are (48 x 47 x 46)/(3 x 2) = 17,296 possible flops. 1 x 1 x 46 = 46 of them will give Justin quads. Probability of Justin flopping quads in this particular hand = 46/17,296 = 0.27%; Odds = (17,296/46) = 375:1. More likely, but still very improbable.

Recognizing when you are behind is something that will take practice and experience. As you learn the game and begin to pay careful attention to your opponents' tendencies, the texture of the flop (overcards, connecting cards, suited cards, pairs, etc.), and what action is taking place before and after you act on your hand, you will be much better able to estimate where you stand.

When playing against timid players like Peter, make sure to give them a little more credit for bets and raises. They will usually show you a strong hand when they play strong. Also be aware of more aggressive players such as Mick and Justin. Don't over-estimate the strength of their hands when they raise or re-raise. They will constantly be trying to take you off of your good hands and even your great hands.

Lastly, make sure you read the board carefully. A paired board is often trouble to your top pair or straight or flush. Suited cards are also dangerous for your straight, and connected cards can be bad news for your top pair/top kicker. We're not telling you to throw your hand away at the first sign of trouble, however. We just want to make sure you're not giving away too many bets when it is pretty obvious that your hand is second best—or worse.

The Money You Lose Not Taking the Other Players Into Consideration

Some players, when they're dealt pocket aces, feel that the hand is over; the only thing left to determine is how large of a pot they're going to win. As previously mentioned, pocket aces do *not* win every time. Consider this hand, played by Chris. Chris considers himself a very unlucky player. He was in the big blind in an $8-$16 hold'em game, and upon looking at his cards, was pleased to see A♠A♣. The hand was folded to Aaron, in middle-position, who raised. Michelle, the cutoff, made it three bets, and Justin, who was on the button, cold-called the three bets. Chris *capped* the pot (made the final raise), so four players saw the flop for four bets each. There was $128 in the pot (four players bet $32, the small blind, who folded, contributed $4, and the house raked $4).

The flop came K♥9♥8♦, giving Chris an overpair. He bet, of course. Aaron called, but Michelle again raised. Justin called the two bets, but then Chris made it three bets, and everyone called. There was now $224 in the pot.

The turn was the Q♣. Chris looked at his hand, knew he had an overpair, and that the flush didn't make it. So he bet $16. Aaron raised to $32. Michelle called. Justin folded and Chris just called. *Maybe one of the players flopped a set of kings*, he thought. The pot now totaled $320.

The river was the 8♠. Chris surmised that the river card didn't help his opponents, so he bet $16. Aaron raised, loudly exclaiming "RAISE," to $32. Michelle re-raised to $48. Chris looked at the huge pot (now totaling $416), and called. Aaron now capped the betting, and Michelle and Chris both called. Aaron showed J♥T♥ for a king-high straight. Michelle turned over 9♦9♠ for a full house (nines full of eights) and scooped the huge $512 pot. Chris then exclaimed, "I can never win with aces!"

Yes, Chris was unluckily outflopped, but this was a hand that he could have (and should have) gotten away from. Let's look at the action on every *street* (betting round).

Pre-flop, you can't argue with Chris' actions. He has the best possible hand and he's going to be out of position after the flop. Capping the betting here is mandatory. But he shouldn't like the flop (K♥9♥8♦). There are two hearts (Chris didn't have the A♥), and the hand connected with players holding cards in the *playing zone*.[9] This was a potentially dangerous flop. Chris was correct to bet the flop, but he must be wary. He needed to recognize that when he was raised, he might be in trouble. While a re-raise (Chris's action) was reasonable (especially as an isolation play against his opponents), Chris desperately wants a small non-heart to come on the turn.

The Q♣ on the turn was another bad card for Chris. If one of his opponents was playing JT, he was now facing a straight. Chris noticed the flush draw on the flop, but didn't notice the straight draw. He also ignored the possibility of one of his opponents holding a set. However, his bet here was reasonable. He needed to find out where he stood.

Aaron told him *exactly* where he thought Chris stood—at best, second place. This player raised a hand where the big blind had been betting (or raising) each street, and where the cutoff had raised on the flop. He had to have a big hand: two pair, a straight, or a set. With this much action there was no chance of a bluff. When Michelle (the cutoff) calls, she's announcing that she has a good hand as well. Perhaps she's on the flush draw (Chris's best-case scenario) or maybe she flopped a set or two pair. Chris should have folded here on the turn (this was his first legitimate opportunity to get away from the hand). He figured to have few outs (he was actually *drawing dead—he had no outs*).

---

[9]In hold'em, especially limit hold'em, many players will play any two cards nine or higher, especially if they're suited.

When the board paired on the river (8♠), Chris should have realized he was likely dead. The only hands he was ahead of were two pair, and *both* of his opponents would have to hold two pair. Assume that Aaron turned two pair (say he held K♦Q♦). Which two pair could Michelle hold? If she held K8 or 98, she just made a full house. Only if she held specifically K9 would Chris be the winner. And that's *only* if Aaron held KQ.

Now consider the betting on the river. Chris foolishly bet (he should have checked). His two opponents raised and re-raised. They're saying that they can beat Chris's strong hand. Even if the pot is $416, if your chance of winning is 0%, throwing *any* money into the pot is incorrect. And with *two* players raising, the chance of *both* players bluffing was zero. Here was yet another chance for Chris to get away from his hand. He called, and then called the final raise (his last chance to leave the hand).

Chris ignored his opponents and paid the price. Yes, he was unlucky that he lost with AA, but his chance of winning with aces against his opponents' actual holdings (including the button, who folded T♠T♣ on the turn) was 64% pre-flop, 4% on the flop, and 0% on the turn. Aces don't win every hand.

In this chapter we examine how you lose money when you ignore your opponents and when you ignore their tendencies. Betting and tendencies work together. In the above example Chris ignored his opponents' betting and paid the consequences. Sometimes, though, you need to know how your opponents act in order to determine what their bets mean.

For example, when a maniac like Mick bets, it simply means that he holds two cards. When he raises, he holds two cards. When he re-raises, he holds two cards. You can't *ever* figure out what Mick holds by his bets. On the other end of the spectrum, when a very tight player like Jerrod calls, he has a good hand. When he bets or raises, he has a great hand; when he re-raises, he has the nuts.

While you will find opponents whose behavior matches these extremes, most of your opponents will fall in the middle. They will bet their good hands, fold their bad hands, and muddle through the rest. However, almost all players will exhibit certain situational betting tendencies. Every player has their own style, and recognizing that style is paramount to winning poker.

Experts have a methodology of describing how poker players think (and act). First level players consider *only* their hands. They ignore (or don't consider) opponents' actions. At the second level, players do think about their opponents' bets and hands when acting. For example, Ray knows that Steve bluffs a lot, so he tailors his actions for that. The third level includes reverse psychology, such as the "I know that you know that I know" conundrum. For example, Steve tailors his actions to Ray's responses to his actions. Fourth level thinking is when Ray adapts his actions to how he thinks that Steve will change his responses to Ray's responses to Steve's initial actions. Whew, this is getting confusing!

You needn't go beyond the second level to be successful at the low and middle limits. Always consider what your opponents are doing *if they are considering what they're doing*. What do we mean by that? Well, let us introduce Mrs. Goldman.

We've all met players like Mrs. Goldman. She's one of the new converts to poker, and her husband (who is, in Las Vegas parlance, a *whale*—someone with lots of money to spend on gambling) has hired a poker tutor for her. She tries hard to understand the game and perhaps in a few years she'll be a better player, but for now she's lost at a poker table. Unfortunately for her opponents, she sometimes stumbles into the winning maneuver. Here's a hand that she recently played in an $8-$16 game.[10]

Chris raised in early position, and Peter immediately re-raised. Jerrod called from the small blind. Mrs. Goldman looked down at her cards. She was in the big blind and held 7♦3♥. Her instructor had been teaching her all about defending the blind with good cards. While we would quickly fold, she quickly called because she realized she *could* make a straight. Chris then made it three bets and Peter immediately made it four bets. Jerrod called, and Mrs. Goldman, remembering an earlier lesson on pot odds, just *knew* that defending was right. So after hesitating for a few moments (not that any of her opponents noticed) she called. The pot was up to $124 ($32 × 4 − $4 rake).

The flop came Q♥3♣2♠. Jerrod checked. Mrs. Goldman had no idea what to do. She had middle pair, but she was facing two raises.

---

[10]While the authors have made Mrs. Goldman a woman, there are many, many male players just like her.

But she remembered the words of her instructor, "…bet when you hit the flop." So she bet $8. Chris raised, and Peter immediately re-raised. Jerrod folded and Mrs. Goldman called.

Chris now had a decision to make. He glanced again at his cards, A♠A♣. He thought for a moment about just calling to disguise his hand, but then decided that the flop was good and he was leading. So he capped the betting. Peter looked at his cards, A♦A♥, and hesitated only for a moment before calling. He didn't think that Chris held pocket queens, but he wasn't thrilled with this hand. Peter began studying Mrs. Goldman, trying to figure out what she held as she threw in the final $8 of the betting round. The pot was up to $220.

The turn was the 9♥. Mrs. Goldman still had a piece of the board, so she bet. Chris still had his pocket aces, so he raised. Peter didn't like what was going on but couldn't see folding his aces when the board read Q♥3♣2♠ / 9♥, so he called. Of course Mrs. Goldman called. The pot was now $316.

The river was the 7♣, giving Mrs. Goldman two pair. She checked, remembering that her instructor told her to check raise when she held strong hands. Chris bet, and Peter called. Mrs. Goldman also called, but then remembered that she was supposed to raise. "Can I raise?" she asked the dealer. After being told she couldn't, she flipped over her two pair (sevens and threes) and took down the $364 pot.

We won't repeat Chris's tirade—suffice to say, he couldn't believe Mrs. Goldman called three bets with 73o. "I can't believe I lost $112!"

Because of all the new players in the games today, you *will* lose quite a bit of money to the Mrs. Goldmans of the world. It's unavoidable. They will play hands that no sane poker player would play. They'll make moves that defy logic, sanity, and reason. You'll be left scratching your head and muttering to yourself.

However, for every hand that Mrs. Goldman wins, she'll lose several more. Her 73o will flop one pair and won't improve, and the aces will win. Or she'll go for the double inside straight draw and miss. Or, well, you get the idea. *While the Mrs. Goldmans of the world do give you bad beats, they'll be the ones who pay you off time after time when you hold the winning hand.* Welcome these players. Sympathize with them when they miss their one-outers (as they usually will). Congratulate them when they crack aces (which, every so often, will happen), even if they're yours. If you treat Mrs. Goldman with kindness, she'll stay in your game longer, increasing your potential win.

Mrs. Goldman stayed in the hand because she thought that it might be good. She's not a *calling station* though. Her actions defy *all* reason. Calling stations, like Chris, will stay in the hand until the end *no matter what*. You can't bluff these players, because they just *know* you're trying to fool them and they might have the best hand. Some calling stations only play good starting hands, while others, such as Michelle, are loose players. No matter, they'll keep calling and calling and calling because they *know* you're trying to pull a fast one. Remember, you can't bluff calling stations.

But they can be *value bet* (betting with the best hand with the knowledge that you will be called by your opponent). And you should be able to win a lot of money from the Chrises and Michelles of the world.

When you sit down at a table, begin to characterize your opponents. Take notes (surreptitiously if you're in a cardroom) about their styles of play. When we sit down at a table where we know no one, we focus on the player with the most money first, as he's usually the biggest threat.

Don't worry if you aren't able to figure out everyone on your first attempt. Just focus on your opponents instead of watching the ball game on television, and you *will* get a read on at least one of them.

You may notice that over time your opponents may change their behavior. You might face Aaron, who has begun to vary his play. It's quite annoying when your opponents start doing the right things. Luckily, we can change our notes on players.

But what if you're facing a table of Nolans, who are good players capable of deceptive moves? We cover this in Chapter 16, *Losing Because You Don't Use Game Selection*, beginning on page 138. For now, common sense gives us the answer—if you're the worst player at the table, it's time to find another game.

A common problem is the lack of knowing the tendencies of your opponents. We always assume that our opponents are good players *relative to the game they're playing*. Because we like to get reads on our opponents, we tend to play quite tight (against the unknown players) until we have an idea of how they play.

A lot of people use stereotypes to classify opponents. For example, Asian players have been considered to be gamblers, conservative dressers play conservatively, Las Vegas tourists play poorly, and young kids bluff a lot. Stereotypes have gotten a bad rap in the United States because many have been used to further racism. We don't favor racial stereotypes in any way, but many poker stereotypes have a basis in fact. Lots of Asian players play a loose, gambling style at the poker table. Many conservative dressers play conservatively. Quite a few Las Vegas tourists don't play poker well in Las Vegas. And many young kids bluff too much.

Should you use stereotypes? Humans, by nature, always stereotype; we have too much information to remember daily if we don't. We look out the window and see the wind blowing branches of the trees, so we grab a windbreaker. We don't even think about the decision—we associate "heavy wind" with "windbreaker."

Stereotyping at the poker table carries a risk, though. Many people use stereotypes against others. We know plenty of Asian poker players who are conservative. Some even give off the *image* (or perception) of being a gambler but actually rarely gamble. They're relying on the fact that *humans act based on their perception of reality, not the reality itself.*

That's an important concept you should remember. Here's an interesting example from the real world. Horace Stoneham, the owner of the New York (baseball) Giants, was asleep at his office at the Polo Grounds when window washers awakened him. He saw all the water streaming down the windows, and assumed it was raining. So he cancelled the doubleheader scheduled for that day. Those are the only two baseball games ever postponed by "rain" on a beautiful, sunny day.[11]

What does that have to do with poker? Stoneham assumed that the water streaming down the windows meant it was raining (a natural assumption). But had he glanced a bit harder (or looked out the windows) he would have noticed the brilliant sunshine. Be wary

---

[11]Before the start of a baseball game, the home team is responsible for postponing the game if there's inclement weather.

about your first assumption of how your opponents play. For example, when we travel to Las Vegas, we tend to dress like tourists (wearing logo polo shirts, for example). We don't play like tourists, but we *look* like tourists.

Let's examine one final example before we conclude this chapter. Aaron is a solid, aggressive limit hold'em player. This particular hand was played against Nolan. They were heads up on the turn in an $8-$16 hold'em game, and Nolan held 7♠7♣. Nolan had raised pre-flop from the cutoff seat and Aaron had called from the big blind. The flop came 8♠5♣3♦. Aaron checked the flop, Nolan bet, and Aaron called. The turn was the 3♣. Aaron checked, Nolan bet $16, and Aaron check-raised. Nolan was pondering his decision.

Nolan knew that Aaron was an excellent player. But he couldn't figure out what Aaron could hold where the 3♣ would improve his hand. Could he have an overpair? Perhaps, but he likely would have raised pre-flop. Could he have a 3? That wasn't likely. Nolan considered that A3 was a distant possibility, but then he rejected that. Could he have 88 or 55? He was representing one of those hands. But Nolan didn't stop his thinking there. He knew that Aaron was capable of making a move, and pondered what Aaron might do holding, say, A♣T♣. Might he not check-call the flop, and check-raise the turn if he hit his one of his overcards or made his flush draw? Nolan felt that was a strong possibility, too. After pondering his play, Nolan called.

The river was the anti-climatic 2♥. Aaron bet, Nolan called, and Aaron sheepishly turned over his A♣Q♣, and Nolan's pocket 7s won the pot. Nolan didn't assume that Aaron had him beat, because he knew that Aaron could make a move. Nolan likely would have folded to a tight player like Jerrod who doesn't make moves.

In poker, *everything* is situational. Players who tell you they would never fold pocket aces have a hole in their game. Sometimes a hand that's worth a raise against one player should be folded against another, given the exact same betting. How would you know this? If you watched your opponents' actions and took notes on your opponents (revising them when necessary), you would. Of course, you must also possess the conviction to act based on your notes. If you practice second-level thinking—always considering the actions of your opponents—you *will* be a step ahead.

The Money You Lose Making Incorrect Bets in Big-Bet Poker

Aaron is a very good limit hold'em player. He's made a nice hourly rate over the past five years and he is confident in his game. Lately however, it seems that everyone wants to play no-limit and pot-limit hold'em instead of limit. Naturally, Aaron has decided that he can make the adjustment and start making money in these big-bet games.

But Aaron is having a very difficult time making any money. In fact, he's regularly losing money. A sample hand might give us some insight.

Aaron is in early position with Q♠Q♥ in a $2/$5 blind no-limit hold'em game. The maximum (and minimum) buy-in for this game is $200. The game just started, so everyone's stack is about the same. Aaron decides to raise to $20. One player in late position cold-calls the raise, as does the big blind. There is now $62 in the pot (minus the rake).

The flop is great for Aaron: Q♣A♦3♦. A set in no-limit hold'em is the most common way to win an entire stack of chips from an opponent. Aaron is already counting up the win in his head. But he doesn't want to lose his opponents, so he bets $20 again.

Shifting perception for a moment, let's look at the hand through the eyes of Michelle. She's our late position caller in this hand, and she holds T♦9♦. The pot is about $80, and it's $20 to her. Although Michelle is a loose player, she does understand pot odds. She knows that she's got a much better chance than 4 to 1 to make her flush, so she makes the easy call.

Peter is the big blind who defended for the additional $15. He has A♣J♣ and his call wasn't that far out of line. Knowing that Michelle can sometimes be a calling station, and also knowing that Aaron would bet regardless of the flop, he decides to test the waters. He raises the bet to $40, doubling Aaron's bet.

When the betting is back to Aaron, he's looking at a pot of $140. It's only $20 to call, and he's pretty sure that if he just calls, he can bring Michelle along for the ride and win a big pot, so he just calls. Michelle calls the additional $20 as well, and they see the turn with $180 in the pot.

The turn is an interesting card: J♠. Aaron still believes he has the best hand, and the possible straight draw doesn't scare him. He decides that he wants to keep his opponents in for the river and comes out with a small bet of $40. He has now committed half of his stack on this hand.

Michelle sees the pot of $220, and with only $40 to call, she decides to take the better than 5 to 1 odds to chase her flush. She has also invested half of her stack.

Peter didn't like the call from Aaron and Michelle on the previous round, but he loved the turn card. Deciding to play this one slow, he calls the $40. There is now $300 in the pot, and the three players go to the river.

The river is the 8♦. With the pot of $300, Aaron confidently fires his remaining $100 into the pot, expecting to take it down right there. But to his surprise, Michelle calls the $100 without hesitation.

Peter sees this and understands that his aces-up probably isn't good. Michelle might be a calling station, but she also commits her money only with a solid hand. Although the pot is $500, Peter decides to save his remaining $100. Even with 5 to 1 odds, if you think there is no chance you are ahead, you should fold.

Aaron tabled his hand and then watched in horror as Michelle turned over her cards for the winning flush. "You called all that way with just a flush draw?!" he shouted. "It's just like Hellmuth says, 'they always draw against you.'" He reached into his pocket for another $200.

In this rather obvious example, it is plain to see where Aaron went wrong. He made small bets into a large pot and gave his opponents the chance to draw to hands on a good but threatening flop. Not only was there a flush draw on the board, but the turn card brought a straight draw as well. Still, Aaron continued to bet small enough to give his opponents the correct odds to call.

As intuitive as it might seem, these small bets are very common in today's no-limit and pot-limit games. The reason for this is twofold. First, most players playing in these games have been playing limit hold'em for most of their poker-playing careers. No-limit games have again come into popularity only recently, mostly due to televised poker. Because of this, players are used to making small bets into large pots because there was no other option. They incorrectly make the assumption that no-limit is quite similar to limit. They're wrong.

The second reason these small bets are so common is because many of today's players were raised on Internet poker. Most online poker software interfaces are equipped with a "Bet" button. This button will make the minimum wager, whether it is a bet or a raise. This is fine for limit poker, but for no-limit and pot-limit poker, this minimum bet or raise is usually a mistake. To see why, let's look at another typical example.

Jerrod, Aaron's friend, often plays on the Internet. When Aaron complained to Jerrod about losing his whole stack with his flopped set of queens, Jerrod replied with a "bad beat" story of his own. Of course, it wasn't a bad beat at all, as we'll soon see.

Jerrod was in the big blind in an online $1/$2 no-limit game. He had a premium hand of A♥K♥. After five limpers plus the small blind, the option was to Jerrod, and he elected to raise. Using the "Raise" button, he made it $4 to go. Everyone called, and with $28 in the pot they saw the flop seven-handed.

The flop was K♦8♣9♥. Jerrod had top pair, and since there was no flush draw to worry about, he fired a confident bet. His error was how he bet. He again used the "Bet" button, so his bet was a measly $2. He was offering the first limper an amazing 15 to 1 on a call, and even better odds to future callers if there was no raise. This was simply asking for trouble, and he got what he was asking for.

Three limpers called the minimum bet, and before the turn there was $34 in the pot ($36 - $2 rake). The turn was the 7♣. Jerrod again used the bet button and bet another $2 into this $34 pot. Justin, one of the limpers, raised. After all, he was holding 7♥ 7♦, and now had a set. Unfortunately for Justin, he also had the bad habit of using the Bet and Raise buttons, and his raise was only to $4. So when the betting got around to Michelle, she was facing a bet of $4 into a $42 pot. Of course there was a chance that Jerrod would raise, but she took the chance to draw to her hand and just called, enjoying odds of better than 10 to 1.

Now fearing he was possibly up against 2-pair, Jerrod just called after the other limper folded. The pot before the river was $48.

The river was the J♦. After being raised on the turn, Jerrod decided to check the river and call if the bet was small. Justin, still sure he had the best hand, now decided to pull the trigger and bet $20 hoping for at least one caller. Michelle raised the bet to $65, putting her remaining chips into the pot. Jerrod disgustingly clicked the "Fold" button, certain that he was beat. Justin called with his set of sevens, but he wasn't as confident as he had been just a second ago.

Sure enough, Michelle turned over Q♣T♥ for the nut straight and took down the $178 pot. Jerrod and Justin both had some choice comments regarding the play of Michelle, who called with nothing more than a straight draw. What these two players didn't consider was the fact that, aside from her questionable pre-flop limp and call, Michelle played the hand quite well.

Both Jerrod and Justin made the fatal mistake of betting and raising too small into a pot that warranted much larger bets. Even a hand as strong as a set is vulnerable to big draws if the price offered is correct, and Michelle was certainly getting the correct price to draw.

In situations where you start out with a premium hand, or when you flop a big hand or draw on a board with drawing possibilities, it is important to bet and raise enough to accomplish your goals. If someone is going to draw to beat you, you want that player to pay too much for his draw, earning you money when that draw is missed (most of the time). You also would like to get as much money into the pot as you can when you are the favorite. Sure, there are times when you would like to chase out certain hands, but for the most part you're looking to build the pot.

In the example above, Jerrod's first mistake was his minimum raise before the flop. Simply doubling the bet wasn't going to increase the pot to any decent amount, and it certainly wasn't going to scare any drawing hands away. After Michelle limped with the questionable hand of QTo, her call of the minimum raise was perfectly justified.

Had Jerrod increased his raise to $14 (instead of the minimum of $2) (which was reasonable given the number of limpers), he might have won the pot right there, or at least thinned the field to the pairs (like Justin's pair of sevens). And had this been the case, a decent bet of *at least half the pot* on the flop would have most likely won it for Jerrod.

Of course, Justin also erred by making the minimum raise on the turn when he hit his set. With the pot of $36, Justin should have raised to about $30. This would have most likely eliminated Michelle with her draw and would have either won the hand right there or caused Jerrod to commit more of his stack with the worst hand. Either way, a large raise here works out for Justin. As it turned out, both Jerrod and Justin made common mistakes that cost them both a nice win.

Now that we've looked at the costly error of betting and raising too little in big-bet poker, let's take a look at the other side of the chip: betting and raising too much.

One of the allures of televised poker is the famed all-in bet. "All-in!" has become the war cry of the newest generation of poker players. The sheer thrill of moving all of your chips into the pot with one double-handed push has made poker the phenomenon that it is today. And lately, players seem to have great difficulty controlling this urge.

Take Joan for example. Joan started to play poker after seeing it on television. After watching Annie Duke and Jennifer Harmon teach their male opponents over and over that poker is not solely a man's domain, Joan decided she too wanted to push the guys around in her local home game, so she asked to play the next time the guys got together. Being the typical men that they were (ego-driven), they salivated at the chance to take Joan's money. Knowing this, Joan spent hours watching tapes of the *World Poker Tour* to prepare for her foray into the world of poker.

The guys had recently switched their home game of Follow-The-Queen and Midnight Baseball to $20 buy-in no-limit hold'em tournaments. Since there were only eight or nine regular players, the mini-tournaments went fast, and they were able to play several in the course of an evening.

In the first event of the night, Joan paid her $20 and took a seat behind Peter, a nice guy but a fairly weak poker player who usually played tight but often lost his patience and sometimes played very speculative hands. Peter was also a player who almost never raised.

With $1,000 in tournament chips, the blinds started at T10 and T20.[12] In the first hand of the evening, Peter limped into the pot for T20. Joan wanted to make her mark quickly, and she was so anxious to make a big move that when she saw the A♠T♣ in her hand, she ignored the size of the blinds and valiantly declared, "All-in!" and shoved her entire stack of T1,000 into the pot.

After a little subdued laughter, everyone folded (including Peter), and Joan took down the tiny T50 pot containing nothing more than the blinds and one call. Although the pot was small, Joan felt the power and rush of adrenalin, and knew that she was destined for glory.

After folding a few hands, Joan found herself in late position with 9♠9♥. After three players already called the T20 small blind, Joan decided it was time to once again show the guys that there was a new sheriff in town, and she wasn't going to stand for any weak limping. Without hesitation, she shoved her whole stack into the pot and again declared that she was "all-in!"

There was more laughter this time, and a few eyes rolled up toward the ceiling, but a few of the players held a look of surprise when

---

[12]In common notation regarding tournament poker, amounts are usually denoted with a capital T instead of a dollar sign. For example, a bet of $2,000 in a tournament is commonly written as T2,000. We will use this notation whenever we discuss hands taken from tournament poker.

quiet Peter uttered, "I call," and turned up K♥K♦. Joan did not hit her miracle two-outer and her tournament life was over just minutes after it started. She would have to wait for the next tournament to begin.

As was the case with betting too little, this error of betting too much or moving all-in is quite common. Check out any online tournament or no-limit cash game, and you will see player after player moving all-in to steal the blinds or to win a small pot on the flop with a monster hand.

This move is usually an error, of course, but do you know why? Let's look at two scenarios that might better explain the problem with the overbet.

In Joan's case, a huge all-in bet before the flop without a huge hand will normally either win a tiny pot or lose a big one. In most circumstances, this bet will only be called by a hand that can beat yours. In the first hand, Joan risked T1,000 to win just T50. She wasn't called, and she won, but was the risk worth it? Not hardly. As she learned in her second hand, risking your whole stack for just a small pot can eliminate you from the tournament. She was only going to get a call from a hand that could beat her. In her best-case scenario, she would be involved in a "coin flip" if a hand like AKo or AQs called her.[13] In tournament poker, it is usually best to avoid these situations so early in a tournament. The risk versus reward ratio does not usually warrant such plays.[14]

The same rule also holds true for players who flop a near lock-hand and bet too much. For example, if you hold a premium hand like Q♣Q♠ and the flop comes Q♦9♥2♣, you are in almost no danger of being out-drawn. A decent bet is fine, especially if you raised pre-flop. Making a bet of about half the pot will look like a standard *continuation bet,*[15] and you will be building the pot as well as enticing players to stick around.

If you make a huge bet of three to five times the size of the pot, the chances of you getting even one caller are very slim. In poker, you

---

[13]Against AKo, an underpair like 99 is a small favorite of about 55-44. Against AQs, the nines are an even smaller favorite of 52-47.

[14]To be fair, Joan did have a 19.2% chance of inflicting a "bad beat" on Peter by having her pair of nines beat Peter's kings. Of course, risking your entire stack when you're a 4.2 to 1 underdog is *not* good poker.

not only need to minimize your losses, you need to also maximize your wins. Blasting willing opponents out of a pot when you flop the nuts is not a good tactic for gaining the most chips from your big hands.

We're certainly not going to cover every aspect of betting in big-bet poker in this one chapter, but we would like to point out that there are times when "overbetting" the pot is a viable strategy. We'll provide two examples.

At times, you may like the strength of your hand, but not enough to let your opponent or opponents see more cards. If you feel it's time to end the hand right now, an overbet (a wager that is typically larger than the pot) might be the solution. Again, this doesn't occur often, and it is not a tactic you want to over-use, but in certain situations it can be your best method of winning the pot.

Another instance when an overbet might be just the thing for you is when you indeed have a strong hand and you are up against a player who calls too much with his weaker hands. For example, you've flopped a set of threes on a board of A♠3♣7♦Q♥2♣, and you believe your opponent has a hand like AT or even aces-up. He'll most likely call even a large bet, so this overbet has become a value bet for you.

Also related to this concept is the deceptive overbet. Many players will overbet the pot as a steal when they have missed their hands. If you are in a game with one or several of these players and they have tried this move, you can make the same play as a value bet when you have a big hand. You're trying to make it look like an overbet steal, but you actually have a hand that will most likely win if called.

Again, the use of the overbet as a no-limit/pot-limit tactic is effective in some scenarios, but it should not be used too frequently. We believe you should be aware of this tactic, however, so you will be able to use it and also defend against it.

---

[15]A continuation bet is a standard bet on the flop made by the pre-flop raiser, regardless of the flop. For more information on continuation bets, read pages 9-19 of *Harrington On Hold'Em, Volume II: The Endgame* by Dan Harrington, as well as pages 277-279 of *Harrington On Hold'Em, Volume I: Strategic Play,* also by Dan Harrington. See Appendix A for more information on these books.

Big bet poker is vastly different from limit poker. There are many more considerations to be made when evaluating a situation, and there are many more opportunities for error. One of the most costly errors is betting an improper amount.

Before you make your bet or raise, think about what you want to accomplish with your play. Do you want to give drawing hands a correct price to make a call, or would you rather protect your strong but vulnerable hand? Do you want to chase players away when you flop a monster, or do you want them to stick around and pay you off? Is the reward of winning a small pot worth the risk of putting all of your chips in play?

Learning the correct betting amounts in big bet cash games and tournaments is a difficult skill to master, but mastering the simple approach of considering your goals before making your move is a big step toward correct decision making and avoiding costly errors. And remember, a mistake in limit poker can only cost you a few bets, but a mistake in big-bet poker can cost you everything.

The Money You Lose With Poor Bluffing Habits

Justin has begun to play no-limit hold'em. As an aggressive limit hold'em player, he made the natural jump into no-limit when it became the game that "all the cool kids" were playing. In no-limit, he found that very large bets could be made to scare his opponents into folding. It didn't matter what cards he held. All he had to do was make a bet large enough to put fear into the heart of the guy across from him, and the pot was his.

Justin became a pretty successful no-limit player, but there was a price for his success.

When the no-limit waiting lists were miles long, Justin would jump into a limit game while waiting for a no-limit seat. Sure, it had been a while since he played limit, but his aggressive style was usually met with lots of chips, so he had no worries. It's too bad, because although Justin didn't know it, no-limit had changed his limit game—for the worse.

While waiting for a seat in the $2/$5 no-limit game one afternoon at the Bellagio, Justin sat in one of the open seats in an $8-$16 limit hold'em game. He had played the $8-$16 many times in the past and he was confident in his ability to kill an hour or two, make a few dollars, and head off into the game where the "serious players" were playing.

Always hungry for action, Justin posted his blind just two spots before his actual big blind would be due. When he saw his first two hole cards of the session, he just knew it was going to be a good day. When the action was to him, he raised to $16 holding A♣Q♣. Two players called: Michelle, a loose/weak player in middle position, and Peter, another loose/weak player on the button. Both blinds folded. After $4 in rake had been taken, the pot was $56.

The flop came 7♥T♥7♦. Justin confidently bet $8. Although he'd missed the flop, he knew that a bet after the flop often takes the pot. Of course, this is much more true in no-limit hold'em as opposed to limit, but Justin was sure it was the correct play. To his mild surprise, both players called. There was $80 in the pot.

The turn card was the T♣. Justin bet out again, but this time Michelle raised. And after thinking for a moment, Peter called the two bets cold. This is when Justin's aggressive instincts took over. Thinking he could bluff his opponents out of the pot, he re-raised. But both Michelle and Peter called. Going to the river, there was now $224 (fourteen big bets) in the pot.

The river was the K♥. This should have been another scary card for Justin (if he was sure neither of his opponents had a ten or a seven for the full house, the only other possible logical holding would have been a flush draw), but since he'd shown great strength on the turn without being re-raised, he decided to make one last bet at the pot. Michelle just called, but this time Peter decided to raise. There was now $288 in the pot (eighteen big bets), and with odds of 17 to 1, Justin decided there was no way he could fold now. So he called, as did Michelle.

Peter turned over his A♥3♥ for the nut flush, and Justin mucked his cards. Of course, as Peter started reaching for the chips, he saw Michelle's cards on the table: T♠9♦ for the winning full house. Michelle took down the $320 pot.

The play by all three players on this hand was atrocious, no doubt, but we'll examine the play of Justin to see where he went wrong.

Raising with his hand was fine. He held a premium hand in early position. His bet on the flop was likely the correct move as well. Both players behind him were loose and weak, and he needed to continue to represent strength, but when they both called on a two-suited and paired board, he should have taken notice.

On the turn, his bet was likely a mistake. With two callers on the paired flop, the chance that one of them had a ten was high, and chasing them both out was unlikely, especially with the flush draw on board. The pot was large, and the correct drawing odds were there.

Still, this bet wasn't his biggest mistake. The worst part of his play was his re-raise of the timid and weak player, Michelle. After Peter calls the two bets cold, there is absolutely no chance that both players (or even one of them) will fold to this bluff raise. The chances of Justin being beaten are near 100%. This bluff has no chance of success.[16] And when Michelle failed to re-raise, the hole Justin was digging for himself became even deeper, as it gave him the motivation to try yet another ill-advised bluff on the river.

Justin carried his no-limit bluffing habits over to his limit game, and it cost him at least five big bets on this first hand alone. How much more do you think Justin's bluffing habits cost him before he realized his errors? The sad ending to this story is that Justin never learned of his mistakes during that session. After losing just short of $500 in the game, Justin's next seat was in front of the television in his living room wondering what went wrong. He never made it to the no-limit game because he no longer had enough for a full buy-in.

Justin's problem isn't uncommon. Even players who have never played no-limit hold'em bluff too much (or at the wrong times). While there are many reasons for this, the cures aren't so obvious. In this chapter, we'll try to pinpoint the major bluffing mistakes players tend to make. After an example of each, we'll see if we can come up with some ways to patch this deadly leak you may have.

Bluffing errors come in three major categories:

1.   Bluffing too much

2.   Not bluffing enough

3.   Bluffing at the wrong time

Bluffing Too Much

In our first example, we found out that Justin, like so many players, tends to bluff too much. He learned this through playing no-limit hold'em, and then absentmindedly carried it over into limit hold'em. But limit poker is not the only game where it is possible

---

[16]Even in a no-limit game this bluff would have almost no chance of working.

to bluff too much. This is a problem that crosses all borders and can be found in any poker game.

Many new no-limit hold'em players are habitual bluffers. After seeing poker on television, they maintain the misguided impression that the bluff is the most powerful tool a poker player can use, and that it should be used as much as possible. The reason for this is simple. Televised poker has to be exciting to keep an audience. Big bets and bluffs are exciting to watch. Believe us, if the entire final table was televised showing every minute of every hand, the viewing public would shrink 90% before the next air date.

Poker is a boring game, for the most part. New players—especially the young ones—are playing for the thrill and excitement they've seen on television. What they don't realize is that most hands are folded before the flop, and most big bets or raises (in no-limit) aren't called. Still, these action-craving neophytes demand excitement, and they'll bluff at every opportunity to get it. Don't be one of those players.

And speaking of those players, let's check out a hand played by Mick. Mick prides himself on what he considers to be his expert bluffing skill. We'll see just how expert Mick really is.

Mick is playing in a typical $500 fixed buy-in no-limit game. With blinds of $2 and $4, he is first to act from early position and decides to raise to $15 with his A♦K♠. Nothing wrong so far. Chris is holding 4♦4♥ and decides to call the bet from middle position. Luckily (for every player at the table), Mrs. Goldman is in the game. She's the big blind in this hand and holds Q♠7♣ (a perfectly respectable hand by her standards), and decides to call the extra $11. After the rake is taken, the pot is $40 and they see the flop three-handed.

Although the flop of 3♥9♠7♥ isn't scary, Mick has completely missed. Still, he continues to show strength and decides to make a continuation bet of $20, which is another perfectly reasonable play on this flop. Chris only has about $100 before the start of this hand (both Mick and Mrs. Goldman have over $500 each in front of them), and if he makes this call he'll have only $65 left. After thinking for a moment about what his opponents might have, he decides to just call. Mrs. Goldman is rather pleased at flopping middle pair and calls as well. There is $100 in the pot.

The turn is the 5♥, potentially completing the flush draw. Mick ignores this possibility and elects to bet $25. It's a very small bet for the pot size, but neither Chris nor Mrs. Goldman seems to notice. Chris calls, and in an uncharacteristic moment, Mrs. Goldman actually folds. She whispers to her husband, who is sitting next to her, "I just *know* Mick has 6♥4♥!" There is $150 in the pot and Mick and Chris go to the river.

The river is a harmless Q♣. Mrs. Goldman would have made Queens-up, but she *knew* they were no good anyway. Mick cuts out sixteen red chips ($80) and shoves them forward. He didn't even notice that Chris only had $40 in front of him. Nor did he notice that Chris has a hard time folding any hand at all. Chris calls the $40 getting 9.5 to 1 on his money, fully expecting to lose. He's shocked when his fours hold up for the $230 pot.

Mick was furious, but he brought it on himself. Had he realized that his last bluff bet was completely ill-timed, he could have saved that last $40. And had he observed Chris's play on past hands, he would know that Chris would call through the river with just about any pair, but never with anything less.

You may have heard the saying, "you're only going to get a call if you're beat" (recall the all-in bets of Chapter 6, *The Money You Lose Making Incorrect Bets in Big-Bet Poker*, beginning on page 46). Well, this was one of those times.

While we can't fault Mick for his play on or before the flop, his turn bet was poor. It was a small bet in relation to the size of the pot, and even worse, it was on a "drawing board," with several straights and flushes possible.

Bluffing when it's obvious that you're going to be called is a very foolish way to play poker, yet we see it again and again. Aggression is fine, and is usually the correct way to play. But timing is a big component of aggression. Without it, bluffing ceases to be effective. And bluffing must remain an effective part of your poker toolbox. Although the game of poker has changed considerably, and bluffing isn't nearly as important as it once was, the art of the bluff still holds its place.

Not Bluffing Enough

One very common error of players who discover that there is actually a correct way to play poker is that they don't bluff enough. In fact, some players don't bluff at all. When a player reads a poker book or two, starts playing tight and aggressive, and begins to see a profit, often he will neglect to be a little creative. Not only is poker a game of people and money, it is also a game of situations. You've no doubt heard the phrase "pick your spots." Not only does this apply to choosing the right hands in which to make a stand, but also when it comes to bluffing. Straightforward play will usually earn you the money, but it can also make you quite predictable. And when your opponents can easily read you, it has a very negative impact on your bottom line.

Peter plays mostly online, and although he plays too many tables at times, he is still a break-even player. He never has very big winning sessions, and his losing sessions are also kept to a minimum. Peter needs to step up his game in some areas. Bluffing is one of them.

Peter was playing in an online $3-$6 limit hold'em game. After only Chris had limped, Peter raised with K♦Q♦, and everyone else folded to Chris who made the call. Going into the flop, there was $12 in the pot minus the rake.

The flop came 2♥4♣T♠ and Chris checked. After missing the flop, Peter also checked.

The turn brought the J♦ and Chris checked again. After pausing for just a second, Peter checked a second time as well.

The river was the 6♣, and once again, Chris checked. But with his hand still unimproved, Peter checked a third time, and when Chris turned over A♥8♥, his ace-high was good enough to win the small pot.

Could Peter have won the pot? We'll never know, since he never took advantage of several situations where he could have bluffed. There were actually three such situations, and Peter failed to act on all of them.

On the flop, Chris showed weakness by checking to the raiser. The flop wasn't scary, and Peter probably should have bet. Even if he was called, he had two overcards and a backdoor straight draw to fall back on.

On the turn when Chris checked again, Peter should have recognized the situation. Chris was most likely weak (most players, after checking the flop and then the turn, have nothing), and a bet here would have most likely won the pot. The turn also gave Peter eight more outs with his open-ended straight draw, so a call here by Chris wouldn't have been a disaster. This type of bluff, when the bettor has a good draw, is called a *semi-bluff*. It's simply a way to value-bet a draw and potentially win the pot uncontested. However, Peter decided to just check.

The river was a meaningless card. Unless Chris had limped in with a pair of sixes, the hand hasn't changed. And when Chris checks for the third time, a bluff bet from Peter was most likely going to take down the pot. But he again checked behind Chris and lost to a lone overcard. As we can see, a bet at any time in the hand from Peter would likely have won him the pot. Although it was a small pot, your hourly rate depends on every pot you win, regardless of the size.

Nolan, on the other hand, understands these concepts. He takes advantage of every situation he spots, and his profits show him to usually be correct. This next example compares Peter to Nolan. It shows just how much proper bluffing habits can influence the outcome of your session and ultimately, your hourly rate.

Nolan is on the button in a $2/$5 no-limit hold'em game. Peter is two seats to the right of Nolan. Both players have had a successful session after about three hours of play, and they are the two biggest stacks at the table, especially since several players have gone broke and new players have taken their places.

After two players limp for $5 (both of whom are new players), Peter decides to raise the pot to $25 holding A♠J♠. Nolan holds T♣9♣ and is about to fold, but he notices that both limpers are holding four red chips in their hands, obviously waiting to make the call. Nolan likes his potential odds and cold-calls the $25. The big blind calls as well, and as expected, so do the two limpers. They see the flop five-handed with $127 in the pot minus the rake.

The flop is 8♦Q♥6♣. The big blind mucks his cards without even checking (the sign of a true professional), and both limpers check. Peter decides to check as well. He wants to see what Nolan does first, as he knows Nolan will take a shot at the pot if he senses weakness most of the time. But to Peter's surprise, Nolan checks too. With his double-gutshot straight draw, Nolan has decided that he can make more money if his straight hits on the turn than he would if he bet out here on the flop. Further, he considers that Peter or one of the limpers might actually have a part of the flop, so he elects to take the free card.

The turn brings the 5♦. Both limpers check again, and Peter decides to bluff with a $15 bet. To Nolan, this looks like a feeler bet, not showing much strength at all. And with the excellent odds Peter is offering, Nolan calls the $15, intending to bet the river if nothing scary comes up. Both of the limpers fold. Going into the river, there is $157 in the pot.

The river is the 2♦, making a flush possible. Peter decides to bet again, and shoves four $5 chips into the pot. This is a fairly suspicious bet to Nolan. Although there is a good chance that Peter has a real hand, Nolan believes that Peter is weak enough to fold his hand to some pressure. Although he has missed his draw, the board has straight and flush possibilities, and he feels that there is an opportunity to take the pot with a bluff raise. And he does just that. With a stern exclamation of, "I raise," he slides one complete stack of twenty red chips forward—a raise to $100. Peter, obviously disgusted, folds. "Nice river," he says.

Yes, it was a nice river card for Nolan. Although it didn't improve the strength of his hand at all, it did improve his situation and position. Nolan is a strong enough player to recognize this and take advantage.

And what mistakes did Peter make in this hand? For starters, he failed to bet the flop. While it would have been a bluff, a continuation bet shows strength most of the time, and after both limpers had checked, a strong hand would naturally bet in this spot. On the turn, Peter finally decided to take a stab at the pot with a bluff, but his bet was far too small. With three opponents and lots of draws on the board, he was giving any drawing hand the right price to call. And on the river, although a runner-runner flush wasn't likely, his bet was again ill-timed and too small. A larger bet might have taken the pot, but Nolan saw the bluff for what it was, and re-bluffed correctly to take down the pot. Nolan understands proper bluffing technique, and Peter could certainly learn a few things from watching Nolan play.

Spotting and exploiting habitual bluffers is not difficult. They are always taking shots at the pot, always raising and re-raising with almost any two cards, and always betting when their opponents show any signs of weakness. These players often build up big stacks quickly, but by the end of the session, they're usually broke. They don't know when to stop bluffing, and since they overuse this poker weapon, they are typically losing players.

Bluffing at the Wrong Time

Other players bluff with a good frequency, but they bluff at the wrong times. When a player has re-raised before the flop, bet the flop, the turn and the river, a bluff-raise is not going to make them fold. Bluffing is a powerful tool, but it must be used with *discretion* and *timing*.

Other situations occur where a bluff has almost no chance of success. Often, a bluff on the river into a habitual calling station will elicit a call with hands as weak as ace-high (and we've even seen calls with hands less than that!). Another bad time to bluff is from early position in a multi-way pot. If a river card comes that could complete an odd straight or flush, betting in this spot is not a good strategy even if no one has been betting during the hand. You'll only get called by a hand that beats you, and more often than not, you'll be raised.[17]

Not bluffing at all is also a mistake. Part of playing solid poker is recognizing certain situations and acting on them. Following up a raise on a non-scary flop against only one opponent is a good spot for a bluff. After several opponents continue to show weakness, a bluff bet will often take down a pot. Looking for these situations (they come up more than you might think) is an essential skill in playing good poker. Finding them and acting on them will only serve to make you a better player. As can be seen in our examples, Nolan is adept at these skills. You should be too, because there are a lot of Peters out there just waiting to send their chips to you in buckets.

---

[17]Don't confuse this situation with Nolan's bluff raise on the river in the last example. He sensed weakness from a bettor, not a draw from a caller.

The Money You Lose Making Mechanical Errors

Consider the following hand, played by Chris. Chris is a decent player, and he understands pot odds. Chris was in a $1/$2 blind $100 fixed buy-in no-limit hold'em game, and had raised to $10 on the button with A♠Q♠. Only the big blind, Joan, called him. Both Chris and Joan had $100 in their stacks when this hand began.

The flop came J♠T♠5♣, giving Chris the nut flush draw and an inside straight draw. Joan checked and Chris made a continuation bet of $15. To Chris's surprise, Joan immediately raised all-in. Chris quickly called.

In some casinos, the cards are turned face-up in cash games when players are all-in. However, in this particular cardroom that wasn't the rule, so the cards were not exposed to the table. Joan did show Chris her hand, A♣K♣, and Chris showed Joan his hand. Chris needed to hit a king (to give him a straight) or a spade in order for him to win the pot. The turn was the J♥ and the river was the T♦. Chris muttered to himself, "I missed *another* draw!" as he threw his cards into the muck. Joan smiled and took down the $200 pot.

Have you noticed the error Chris made?

In hold'em, the best five-card hand wins. Both Chris and Joan had *identical five-card hands*: they both had two pair, jacks and tens, with an ace kicker. The fact that Joan's *sixth* card was a king versus Chris's queen was irrelevant. But Chris threw his cards into the muck, so his hand was dead and Chris lost $100 needlessly.

In this chapter we examine errors of commission—mechanical mistakes that needlessly cost poker players money. Besides mucking winning hands, other such errors include: acting out of turn, making a motion that is interpreted as a check (or bet), clicking the wrong button (in online poker), making incorrect verbal declarations, intending to raise but throwing out a single, large-denomination chip, and misreading your hand. The thread that links all of these errors is a lack of situational awareness.

Consider Mrs. Goldman. At least she *knows* that she doesn't know everything. Somehow she has grasped only portions of what her professional teacher has told her— usually with disastrous results. Here we find her playing in a $1/$2 blinds $100 fixed buy-in no-limit hold'em game. This was the first hand of a new game, so every player had $100 in chips. Mrs. Goldman was on the button holding T♦T♥. Michelle had limped from early position, as did Joan and Chris. Mrs. Goldman decided that her hand was worth a raise, so she threw a $5 chip into the pot.[18] Jerrod in the small blind folded and Peter, in the big blind, checked his option. Five players saw the flop (with $10 in the pot).

When the dealer pushed Mrs. Goldman her $3 change (from her call), she asked why it wasn't a raise. The dealer explained that she didn't say "raise," so her single, higher-denomination chip was considered a call. Mrs. Goldman compounded her first mistake by alerting her opponents that she held a hand worth raising.

The flop came Q♠9♦8♦, giving Mrs. Goldman an inside straight draw. Peter checked, and Michelle bet $5. Joan folded, Chris called, and Mrs. Goldman elected to call. After all, she had a draw. Peter also elected to call. After the rake, the pot grew to $29, and four players saw the turn.

The 7♦ came on the turn, adding a flush draw to Mrs. Goldman's outs. Given that she now had two draws, she thought her hand was definitely worth betting, so she bet $20. However, it was Peter's turn to act (Mrs. Goldman was on the button); thus, the dealer pushed Mrs. Goldman's chips back to her and told Peter to bet or check. Peter looked down at his 6♥5♠, and felt that unless Michelle had specifically JT (and he didn't think that was the case), he could check-raise Mrs. Goldman when she bet. After all, his straight was undoubtedly better than whatever hand Mrs. Goldman

---

[18]As we explained in Chapter 6, *The Money You Lose Making Incorrect Bets in Big-Bet Poker*, beginning on page 46, Mrs. Goldman's intended $3 raise (to $5) was far too small.

had backed into. And even Peter, who never raises unless he has a monster, could check-raise in *this* situation.

So Peter, along with the rest of the table, checked to Mrs. Goldman, who saw no reason not to bet, and tossed $20 into the pot. Peter put his plan into action and check-raised another $20 (making the total bet $40). Both Michelle and Joan folded, but Chris called. Mrs. Goldman also called, making the pot $146 as three players saw the dealer put the 6♦ on the river.

Mrs. Goldman thought that her straight was undoubtedly the best hand, and she was about to bet her last $48 in chips when she realized that Peter was first to act. Peter didn't like the river card at all and checked. Chris, who had J♣T♣, didn't like the fourth diamond and also checked. Mrs. Goldman was about to push her last $48 into the pot, and she was nervously tapping her right hand on the table. The dealer saw this and interpreted the action as a check, asking Peter to now show his cards. Mrs. Goldman asked the dealer why she couldn't bet. The dealer told her that he interpreted her hand movement as a check. After the floorman was called (and ruled that the dealer was correct), and before Peter could expose his nine-high straight, Mrs. Goldman exclaimed, "Straight," and turned over her cards. She had forgotten that she also had a flush draw. Chris looked at Mrs. Goldman's T♦T♥ and realized that she had a straight flush. The dealer realized it, too, and pushed Mrs. Goldman the $244 pot, telling her, "You have a straight flush!"

Of course, Mrs. Goldman should have correctly read her hand. However, that's just not one of her abilities. This *should* be one of your capabilities, though. If you are having trouble reading your hands, practice by playing on a free Internet site (almost all of the online poker sites offer free, "play money" games). If you're an Omaha player, you *must* master the ability to read hands. Even accomplished Omaha players know that they occasionally make mistakes. Thus, whenever they have doubts about their hand they table their hole cards (lay them face-up on the table) and let the dealer read their cards. We suggest you do the same.

There were numerous other errors made by these players. The most egregious was Peter's raise of only $20 in a $49 pot. By the time Mrs. Goldman had to act, the pot was $69, and any chance of Mrs. Goldman folding—admittedly, this would be an unlikely occurrence—had gone down the drain.

Two other common errors are string bets and throwing out the wrong size chip—either betting too little or tossing an oversize chip into the pot thinking it will be considered a raise. But when a player bets (or calls) with an oversize chip, the bet is, in almost all casinos, considered a *call* rather than a raise, unless the player has first said "raise." Consider this hand played by Mick.

Mick found himself on the button in the first hand of a brand new $500 fixed buy-in $1/$2 blinds no-limit hold'em game. Jerrod limped under-the-gun. It was folded to Chris in middle position, who also limped. Everyone folded to Mick, who debated raising *blind* (without looking at his cards), but decided to look. He was surprised to see K♣K♠, and in his excitement, threw out a $25 chip. Joan tossed in the extra $1 from the small blind, and Peter checked his option from the big blind. It was then that Mick exclaimed, "Hey, I raised." The dealer told him that an oversize chip thrown into the pot without the player saying raise is considered a call. After the floorman confirmed this, play continued.

The flop came T♣6♣3♣, not a bad flop at all for Mick. Everyone checked to Mick, and Mick decided to suck people into his pot by betting just $10. Joan folded, and Peter began to think. He had 5♣4♣ and he knew he should raise, but worry had him considering the chance that Mick had him beat. So after contemplating his action for a few moments, he threw two $5 chips into the pot, paused, and threw in two more. Jerrod, next to act, said, "Isn't that a string raise?" And the dealer nodded his head in agreement, stating, "Sir, you must make your bet in one motion, or declare the amount of your bet, or say 'raise'; if you say 'raise,' then you can first put out the amount to call the bet, and then put out your raise." The dealer gave back $10 to Peter. Jerrod then called Mick's bet and Joan folded.

The turn was the 9♣. Peter and Jerrod checked, and Mick decided that he needed to bet big and threw out a $100 chip. The dealer correctly announced, "The bet is $100." (After the flop, a player betting with an oversize chip in no-limit bets that amount.) Peter looked at the board, and knew that going for a two-outer was wrong, and folded. Jerrod peered at his own hand, A♣Q♠, and shoved his chips in. Mick called, and was stunned when Jerrod flipped over his nut flush. The river was an irrelevant 8♥, and Jerrod more than doubled-up to start the game.

Consider what would have happened on this hand had neither Mick nor Peter made any betting mistakes. If Peter makes his raise, it's possible that Jerrod would fold. If Peter makes a substantial raise, Jerrod should fold. Of course, Peter was only going to make a minimum raise (to $20 from $10), and it's likely that Jerrod would call that. However, Mick would almost certainly re-raise Peter, and it's almost certain that such a large raise would cause Jerrod to fold. Peter's action in such a case is harder to determine. He has the best hand, but considering that he's playing scared he would probably fold.

Of course, had Mick raised to $25 pre-flop, this situation would never have happened. Peter would almost certainly fold, although it's possible that Jerrod would call. For the moment, assume that Mick did raise and only Jerrod called. On the same flop (T♣6♣3♣), unless Jerrod moves all-in on the flop, Mick will. It's probable that Jerrod won't call a $475 bet by Mick (after all, Jerrod only has a draw) and Mick will win the hand.

The final error we will mention in this chapter is mis-clicking in online poker. In online poker games, you generally click with the mouse on a button labeled "Bet," "Fold," or "Check." (There are check-boxes too, such as "Raise," "Fold to any Bet," "Raise Any," and "Call Any.") Depending on the site, some of these buttons are *not* large. Additionally, if you are playing on multiple tables, there are more buttons on the screen making it even easier to mis-click in that situation. (See Chapter 11, *Losing Because You Shouldn't be Playing*, beginning on page 98 for other issues regarding playing multiple tables online.)

There's a simple solution to this problem: slow down. Just as players in brick and mortar cardrooms should take their time when acting (to make sure the action they perform is the one they want to perform), make sure your online action is the one you intended to make. Otherwise, you might find yourself raising with 7♣2♠ instead of folding.

Mechanical errors are "dumb" mistakes. They are *all* preventable errors. If you're unsure about whether or not your hand is the winner, let the dealer decide. Slow down, act in turn, and not only will you avoid some errors, you will be more likely to end up a winner.

The Money You Lose Playing
for Only Half the Pot

Assume that you have a choice of playing two poker games. In the first game, you would have the chance to win normal-sized pots, with normal variance. In the second game, you could only win *half* of the same sized pots, with the same variance. Which game would you choose? It's not much of a decision, is it?

Now, what if I told you that you could play in a game that had *half* the normal variance, but you could have a chance to win more money than you would otherwise win? The only catch is that you would have to modify your play a bit in order to decrease your variance.

This sounds too good to be true, but it isn't. In most cardrooms, split-pot games such as Omaha high/low and stud high/low have some of the largest pots and have some of the lowest variance for good players. Yet in most cardrooms today, players who frequent split-pot games play hands that increase their variance *and* limit their winnings.

If you decide to play Omaha high/low or stud high/low, you need the discipline to know which hands to play. In split games, the best high hand wins half the pot, and the best low hand wins half the pot (A2345 is a perfect low, as straights and flushes are irrelevant for low).[19] A low hand must also have five different cards eight or lower; thus, Omaha high/low is also called Omaha Eight or Better or simply Omaha-8. In Omaha high/low, you make both the low and high hands by using *exactly* two cards from your hand and *exactly* three of the five cards on the board. It's definitely an action game at

---

[19]There are some poker games, such as deuce-to-seven lowball, where straights and flushes count against the low hand.

the low limits, as you will see in this hand of $6-$12 Omaha high/low played by Michelle.

Michelle was on the button holding A♥K♦T♥2♦, a rather good hand in Omaha high/low. After four players limped in, she raised. Both blinds and the four limpers called, and seven players saw the flop of 8♠8♣3♣.

This flop gave Michelle the *nut low draw* (a draw to the best possible low hand) and a pair of eights (with an ace-king) for high. Jerrod, in the small blind, bet $6. Chris, in the big blind, raised to $12. The next two players folded. Justin, Peter, and Joan called, too. Michelle elected to call, and Jerrod called Chris' raise.

The turn was the 7♥. Jerrod checked, Chris bet $12, and everyone called. Michelle now had the nut low, so she called, with Jerrod tossing in his $12 as well. The river was the 2♣. Now Michelle's low was *counterfeited*; instead of having the nut low of 7432A, her low was 8732A (the underlines indicate the cards played from a players' hand). The river betting was spirited: Jerrod bet, Chris raised, Justin folded, and Peter and Joan called. Michelle folded, knowing that she wasn't getting any part of the pot, and Jerrod just called. Jerrod showed A♠4♠5♥9♦ for the nut low, Chris showed 8♥7♦6♠5♣ for a full house (eights full of sevens), Peter had A♣2♥4♣T♦ for the nut flush (for which he earned nothing) and another nut low, and Joan had A♦3♦4♥8♦ for a full house (eights full of threes) and yet another nut low. Chris won half the pot, and Jerrod, Peter, and Joan each got one-sixth of the pot.

Michelle unnecessarily lost $24 on this hand. While Omaha experts have been debating the usefulness of pre-flop raises for years, that wasn't the problem with her actions on this hand. Michelle should have folded on the flop, saving herself $24. You may be thinking, *why should Michelle fold when she has the nut-low draw?* And we'll answer that question in a few moments.

The goal in split-pot games is to *scoop the pot* (win both the high *and* the low). Winning half the pot is better than nothing, but it takes winning *many* halves of pots in order to have a winning session. Let's look at the math behind this.

Assume you've won half of an Omaha high/low pot, and the total pot was $200. There were four players in the pot, so each of you contributed $50 to the pot. You won half the pot, so you netted $50 (or a payoff of 1 to 1). If you had scooped the pot, though, you would have won $150 net, for a payoff of 3 to 1. To win as much as you do when you scoop a hand, you must win three halves of pots.

Now, Omaha high/low is known as a "river game." That's not true in the slightest. Yes, players' hands get counterfeited on the river (like Michelle's), but the key in Omaha high/low (and all forms of Omaha) is starting hand selection. This book is not an Omaha strategy book—we're not going to tell you which hands you should play. But we are going to tell you about hands that many players play that you should avoid like the plague.

Correctly played, Omaha high/low is a pre-flop game. Play hands that can scoop and you can win. Play hands that can't and you *will* be donating to the table. This necessitates playing tight. In Omaha high/low, playable hands share one overriding characteristic: they can scoop a hand (excluding play out of the blinds). Good starting hands should have cards that work together: low cards, high cards, or a *playable* combination thereof.

Every Omaha hand has six two-card combinations. Let's look at the best possible Omaha high/low hand, AA23ds (the *ds* indicates that it is double-suited), and compare it with a poor hand, 23s9Q. In the first hand, every combination is working. You have two nut-flush draws and a pair of aces for high, as well as the nut-low draw and the second nut-low draw. Contrast that hand with the second hand. There is only one decent combination of the six in the second hand (32s). The other combinations: 92, Q2, 93, Q3, and Q9, add nothing to the hand. And the "good" combination is the *third nut-low* draw—hardly something to get excited about. The flush draw adds no value to the hand (it's the *worst* possible flush draw). *In Omaha, you want to play hands that have a draw to the nuts (be it high, low or both),* and not much else. The first hand is worth a raise but the second hand should be mucked without thinking.

You are correct in thinking that this doesn't leave many playable hands. In Bill Boston's book, *Omaha High-Low: Play to Win with the Odds,* he analyzes every one of the 5,277 possible starting hands.[20] He comes to the conclusion that "...there are approxi-

[20]Boston, Bill. *Omaha High-Low: Play to Win with the Odds.* Las Vegas: Poker Plus Publications, 2002.

mately 770 hands that show some profit potential, meaning that the remaining 4,462 hands have a negative value."[21] That would mean playing just 14.6% of your hands (excluding blinds). While we have some minor quibbles with his analysis, we agree that most Omaha hands should be thrown away pre-flop.

Yet the average player doesn't look at an Omaha hand in that manner. They look for a hand that has just *one* playable combination (of the six) and will play that hand. But Omaha isn't hold'em. In hold'em, you can play a higher percentage of starting hands because you only need two cards that work together. Omaha high/low is profitable for good players because most of your opponents will play far too many hands.

Several years ago one of the authors developed a rule that covers this situation: *the more cards you are dealt to start a hand, the fewer hands you should play.* When this rule was proposed on rec.gambling.poker, it was hotly debated. Yet the rule should be obvious. In Omaha high/low, ideally you want a hand with six good combinations. In hold'em you need one. Thus, *a priori*, you will play more hands in hold'em than in Omaha high/low.

There is one group of starting hands where the cards work together but should be mucked: middle cards. Say you're dealt 7789ds. Like AA23ds, all of your cards are working together. However, *what nut hands can you make?* If you make the nut straight, you will probably only get half the pot because the nut low will be out against you. You have two flush draws, but neither is the nut flush draw. You can't make the best low. Even if you make the best possible full house, there would be a low out against you. While 7789ds is a good hand for Omaha high-only, it's a lousy hand for Omaha high/low. *Muck your middle card hands and you will be much better off.* Let's look at an example where this advice wasn't followed.

Justin, our "WPT-look" player, was under the gun in a typically loose $6-$12 Omaha game. Justin peered down at 7♠7♣8♣9♠ and knew that he couldn't call with that hand. So he raised. His tactic provided the expected results in this game—four players, including both blinds, called.

---

[21]*Ibid*, p. 8.

The flop came 5♥6♦9♥, giving Justin the nut straight. If the hand ended right now, Justin would scoop the pot. Justin immediately went for his chips to bet, but the dealer pointed out that the small blind, Joan, would act first. Joan peeked at her cards and bet. The big blind, Mick, called. Justin forcefully reached for chips and yelped, "raise 'em up." The next player folded, but the button, Nolan, called, as did both blinds.

The turn was the K♠. Joan and Mick checked and Justin bet, with Nolan, Joan and Mick calling. The river was the Q♣, and Justin felt that it was a safe card. Joan checked, but Mick bet. Justin did see that he no longer held the nuts (a JT would give an opponent a higher straight) but he couldn't see anyone sticking around with *that* hand. So he raised. Nolan shook his head in a resigned way and folded. Joan also folded. Mick quickly re-raised. Justin, now getting a pain in the pit of his stomach, called. Mick turned over A♦4♦T♥J♠, giving him the nuts and the pot. For the record, Joan held A♠2♣3♦7♦, giving her the nut low draw. Nolan had flopped the nut low draw and a set, A♥2♥5♠5♣. Justin then exclaimed, "I can *never* win hands where I flop the nuts."

Justin really only has himself to blame. On the flop, there is *no chance for him to scoop the pot!* Choose any two possible cards for the turn and river, and no matter what you choose, someone will make a low, a higher straight, a flush, or a full house to take *at least half the pot from Justin.* Indeed, Justin was doomed *the moment he played the hand!*

There is a solution to this problem: don't play middle cards. Your good flops are illusory. Trust us, and fold them without thinking. Justin's hand was playable out of the blinds, but we would be wary throughout the hand. *Straights are extremely vulnerable in Omaha.*

The second key to Omaha high/low is to *honestly* evaluate your hand after the flop. Let's assume that you started with A♦A♥2♥3♦, you raise under the gun and all nine players call. The flop comes T♠T♣6♠. The small blind bets and the big blind folds. Should you fold, call or raise?

Pre-flop, you had a great hand; post-flop, your hand is poor. With seven players seeing the flop it's unlikely your two pair (aces and tens) is the best hand. You don't have the spade flush draw. You do have a backdoor nut-low draw, but is that really worth staying in the hand? Your only chance for high is an ace. But an ace is very un-likely to come. *In Omaha high/low, when you hold a pair of aces and almost everyone calls, it's likely that the other two aces are in players' hands.*

Now let's return to the example from the beginning of this chapter. Michelle had raised pre-flop holding A♥K♦T♥2♦. The board came 8♠8♣3♣ / 7♥ / 2♣ and Michelle folded on the river. We commented that Michelle should fold on the flop even though she had the nut low draw.

First, Michelle has no chance for the high portion of the pot. Her only hope is that she makes the low. But will she be the only player with the nut low? *Seven players saw the flop.* It's quite likely that someone else has an A2. Still it might be right to draw out. Let's look at the math.

Michelle needs a 3, 4, 5, or 6 to make her nut low. She has sixteen outs *twice* (both on the turn and on the river, she can catch one of her sixteen outs) on the flop. Her chance to hit the low on the turn is 16/44, or 36.4%. But we need to consider other possible occurrences.

An ace or a deuce could come on the turn, immediately counterfeiting her low. There's a 6/44 (13.6%) chance of that happening. If she makes the low on the turn, there's a chance she'll be counterfeited on the river (6/43), or a net chance of 5.1%. She could also make the low on the river—there's an 18.6% chance (22/44 × 16/43). The table below summarizes the possibilities.

Michelle's Chances of Making Low	
Make Low on Turn, *Not* Counterfeited on River	31.3% (16/44 × 37/43)
Make Low on River, *Not* Counterfeited on Turn	18.6% (22/44 × 16/43)
Chance of Making Low	49.9%
Counterfeited on Turn	13.6% (6/44)
Make Low on Turn, Counterfeited on River	5.1% (16/44 × 6/43)
Don t Make Low	31.4% (22/44 × 27/43)
Chance of *Not* Making Low	50.1%

There's $80 in the pot before the flop (assuming that $4 is dropped for the rake). On the flop, Jerrod (the small blind) bet $6, Chris (the big blind) raised to $12, and three players called. Assuming that Jerrod will simply call the raise, Michelle must bet $12 to win $140. Certainly she has the right price. Can you spot the errors in this reasoning?

There are actually two flaws here. First, Michelle can only win *half* the pot. She must bet $12 to win $70. Second, there's a strong likelihood that someone else holds an A2, so she's only going after a *quarter* of the pot. If that's the case, she's betting $12 to win $35.

Our discussion of this hand would not be complete without considering the implied odds of the river. If the low doesn't come on the turn, Michelle would still have sixteen outs on the river, or a 16/43 (37.2%) chance of making the low on the river. We also must include the chance of her making the low on the turn and being counterfeited on the river, a 6/43 (14.0%) chance. Overall, Michelle should have folded on the flop.

Frequently questioned is the value of an ace in Omaha high/low. *Aces are worth their weight in gold in all high/low split games, especially tight games.* In Omaha high/low, the only way you can make the nut low is to either hold an ace or for an ace to come on the board.

Indeed, there are not many Omaha high/low hands that you should play that don't have an ace. Peter Boston believes there are only about fifty profitable hands that don't include an ace.[22] Yes, you should play 2345, but wouldn't you prefer to hold A345?

Omaha high/low is a game of holding the nuts and having draws to the nuts. Shane Smith wrote of Omaha, "If it's possible, it's probable."[23] In low-limit games, typically five or more players see the flop. That's thirty two-card combinations to mix with the board. Thus, the nuts (unless it's a straight flush or quads) is usually out there.

Stud high/low has its own traps to avoid. Like Omaha, you should only play hands that have the potential to scoop the pot. The two

---

[22]*Ibid,* p. 14.

[23]Smith, Shane. *Omaha Hi-Lo Poker: How to Win at the Lower Limits.* Las Vegas: Poker Plus Publications, 1996, p. 79.

biggest traps that we see are the playing of three random low cards and playing hands suited for stud *high* but not high/low. Here are two hands illustrating these traps.

Justin picked up (J♣Q♠)K♠ (the cards within the parentheses are the players' hole cards), and was second to act after Michelle brought in the action for $3 with the 2♣ in a $10-$20 stud high/low game. The other door-cards (also called up-cards) around the table were the 6♥, 5♠, 2♥, 9♣, J♥, and 9♦. Justin held the highest up-card and three to a straight, and elected to complete the betting to $10. Nolan, holding (4♠7♣)6♥ called; Peter, with (5♥3♣)5♠, also called. Michelle, who brought in the action with (9♠8♥)2♣ threw in the extra $7 so four players saw fourth street.

Everyone caught good cards on fourth street. Michelle picked up the 4♥, giving her (9♠8♥)2♣4♥; Justin received the T♠ giving him (J♣Q♠)K♠T♠; Nolan paired his hole card when he got the 6♦, making his hand (4♠7♣)6♥6♦; and Peter added another low card with the 7♥, making his hand (5♥3♣)5♠7♥. Nolan bet $10, and everyone called, including Justin.

On fifth street the good cards kept coming. Michelle now had four to a low, holding (9♠8♥)2♣4♥7♠; Justin now had both a four-flush and four to a straight, with his hand being (J♣Q♠)K♠T♠6♠; Peter added another low card—his hand became (4♠7♣)6♥6♦A♦; and Nolan made trips, with his hand now (5♥3♣)5♠7♥5♦. Peter bet $20, Nolan raised to $40, and Michelle made the excellent decision to fold. Justin called, although he was a bit worried about Nolan's hand. Peter just called.

Sixth street didn't bring the card that Justin needed. He paired, giving him (J♣Q♠)K♠T♠6♠6♣; Peter made his low, with (4♠7♣)6♥6♦A♦2♠; and Nolan now had a four-low to go with his trips, (5♥3♣)5♠7♥5♦2♦. Peter checked, Nolan bet $20, with both Justin and Peter calling.

Seventh street *appeared* to help everyone:

Justin made two pair, (J♣Q♠)K♠T♠6♠6♣(Q♣);

Peter also made two pair with his low, (4♠7♣)6♥6♦A♦2♠(A♥);

and Nolan made a low to go with his trips, (5♥3♣)5♠7♥5♦ 2♦(A♣).

Peter checked, Nolan bet $20, Justin called, Peter raised to $40, Nolan re-raised to $60, Justin called and Peter called. Nolan's trips and his 7532A low were the best high and low hand and he scooped the pot.

Justin went wrong when he elected to play this hand. While three high cards to a straight may be playable in stud high, it's a trap hand in stud high/low. *You can only scoop if all your opponents don't get a low.* That's very unlikely, and Justin's downhill run on this hand began on third street. Additionally, two key cards were out—two 9s—that reduced his chance of making a straight (a third 9 was one of his opponents' hole cards).

Fourth and fifth streets just gave Justin more reasons to stick around: a straight draw and a flush draw. While a paired door-card isn't as much of a danger sign in stud high/low as it is in stud, it's still not a good thing. Justin didn't even pay attention to this. When he paired up his six on sixth street, he knew that Peter didn't have trips, but he was fighting for only *half* the pot. And Nolan's raise on seventh street was the warning sign that Justin was most likely in trouble. Of course, Justin saves $180 by just throwing away his hand on third street.

It's not as if the play of the other players in this hand was exemplary. Michelle, who had the bring-in, should have folded to the completion bet. Her (9♠8♥)2♣ is almost certainly behind *at least* one of her opponents; more likely, she trails the entire field. Had she folded to the completion bet she would have saved $17. Both Nolan and Peter should have been more aggressive on this hand. Once they make the decision to play their hands (Peter held (4♠7♣)6♥ and Nolan held (5♥3♣)5♠), they should have considered raising to limit the competition. Peter should also have raised when he made his low on sixth street. Poor decisions are quite typical of stud high/low play at these limits.

Not only are three random high cards a poor starting hand, three random low cards are also a poor hand. Consider this hand, solely from Chris's perspective, where he picked up (2♠8♣)5♠. Chris was in the one seat, and Michelle brought in the action for $3 with the 2♦ from the three seat. Peter, with (??)7♦ completed the bet to $10. Jerrod, with (??)4♠ called, Chris made an ill-advised call, and

Mick also called, with (??)3♥. Michelle then folded. The other folded up-cards were the 7♣, Q♠, and 9♥.

On fourth street Chris caught a fourth low card, giving him (2♠8♣)5♠7♥. Mick appeared to catch good with a 2♥ to go with his 3♥. It looked like Peter got a brick when he picked up the J♦ to go with his 7♦. Jerrod also appeared to brick when he received the T♠ to go with his 4♠. Peter was first to act and checked. Jerrod also checked. Chris, looking at Mick's good catch decided to check. Mick bet $10, with Peter and Jerrod calling. Chris thought only for a moment and called. After all, he had a four-low.

Only Chris caught a good card on fifth street (at least by appearances). The hands became: Chris—(2♠8♣)5♠7♥6♠; Mick—(??)3♥2♥K♣; Peter—(??)7♦J♦3♣; and Jerrod—(??)4♠T♠K♦. Jerrod checked, Chris bet $20 (after all, he had a low and a straight draw), with Mick, Peter and Jerrod all calling.

Sixth street didn't help Chris but appeared to help his opponents. The hands now were: Chris—(2♠8♣)5♠7♥6♠J♣; Mick—(??)3♥2♥K♣8♠; Peter—(??)7♦J♦3♣2♣; and Jerrod—(??)4♠T♠K♦T♣. Jerrod bet $20, and everyone called. Chris thought about raising, but it looked like Peter might have a better low, so he elected to just call.

Chris caught the 5♥ on seventh street. He looked again at the other boards, knowing his pair was no good. But he did have a low, so when Jerrod bet $20, he immediately called. Mick thought for a moment and also called, and Peter quickly called. The hands were turned over and Chris saw that he was getting none of the pot. Jerrod showed (6♥6♦)4♠T♠K♦T♣(J♥) for two pair, jacks and sixes. After Chris showed his hand, Mick revealed (4♦5♣)3♥2♥K♣8♠(7♠) for a 75432 low, better than Chris's 87652. Peter then sighed and showed his hand, (3♦A♦)7♦J♦3♣2♣(4♥), for a 7432A low and half the pot. Jerrod and Peter split the pot.

Chris would have saved $80 by folding on third street. Sure, his (2♠8♣)5♠ looked pretty, but it was a hand much better suited for razz (seven card stud for low) than for stud high/low. How was Chris going to scoop with his holding? He needed to catch *three* perfect cards (346, 467, or 679) to make a straight. While it was probable that if Chris caught 346 he would scoop, catching three specific cards isn't likely.

Of course, Chris could easily have caught better cards to make a winning low. However, he started with an 852 low. Two of his opponents started with better lows: Mick with 543 and Peter with 73A. (Also note that both Mick and Peter had excellent scoop potential, Mick with three cards to a wheel and Peter with three to a flush.)

In stud high/low, like Omaha high/low, throw away your poor starting hands. Yes, you will be playing far fewer hands than your opponents. In fact, the only reason that you can make money at the low limits in Omaha high/low and stud high/low is that most of your opponents play anything that remotely resembles a playable hand. Enjoy conversing with your tablemates while playing these games; you'll have plenty of time to do so.

As noted before, this book is not a text on Omaha high/low and stud high/low strategy (we give some references in Appendix B for those who want to hone their skills in these games). For those who do play split-pot games, the easiest method of increasing your win rate is by simply folding a lot more starting hands.

Other Topics

♠ T E N ♥

Losing Because You Don't Have an Adequate Bankroll

Nolan was playing in a $15-$30 limit hold'em game. He had four racks of $5 chips in front of him, as well as several "working stacks," totaling well over $2,000. Chris (you'll remember his bad luck from Chapter 5, *The Money You Lose Not Taking the Other Players Into Consideration*, beginning on page 38) was a friend of Nolan, and they were about to have dinner. Chris stopped at Nolan's table about twenty minutes before their scheduled meet up time. He was grinning and giddy with excitement.

"What are you so happy about?" Nolan questioned his friend.

"Dude, I just crushed that $3-$6 game for almost $300!" Chris replied, sitting down in the one open seat at Nolan's table. He had a mixed rack of $5 and $1 chips, and he pulled a small pile of $5 chips from his pocket and put everything on the felt in front of him.

"Uh, what are you doing?" Nolan asked.

"Playing in the big game, man! What did you think?"

Nolan didn't reply. He knew that Chris was too inexperienced to play in this game, as well as the fact that he didn't have nearly the stake to sit down. It was a bad idea, but Nolan said nothing to help. He knew that any words would embarrass his friend, and he also knew that Chris was stubborn and wouldn't heed Nolan's warnings. He would have to learn on his own.

Nolan didn't want to witness the slaughter of his friend. He put his remaining chips in an empty rack and got up from the table.

"Where you going? With a win like that, I'll bet you're off to the $30-$60 game!" Chris said.

83

"No, I'm calling it a night. I'll see you in twenty minutes for dinner, right?"

"OK, I'll take a break for dinner. I want to play a few hands first. I'm on a roll!"

As Nolan went to the cashier's cage, Chris chose to post his blind instead of waiting for the button to pass. He was anxious to get started. His first two cards were K♦4♠. It wasn't a great hand, but this was his time to shine, and he just *knew* he could make it happen. An early position player three to the right of Chris raised. Chris decided he wouldn't be bullied and decided to re-raise. He didn't recognize any players in this game because it wasn't his usual game, but he didn't think that mattered much. Besides, they didn't know him either. Only one player behind Chris called. He was a tough looking man in his forties, and he had a lot of chips in front of him. The blinds folded, and the original raiser called the re-raise. They went to the flop with $111 in the pot (three players for $30 each, plus the $10 small blind and the $15 big blind, less the $4 rake).

The flop came Q♥7♣K♠. The original raiser checked and Chris, with top pair, bet $15. The tough looking player called the bet, as did the original raiser. There was $156 in the pot heading to the turn.

The turn card was the 4♥, giving Chris two-pair. When the first player again checked, Chris confidently bet $30. But instead of calling, the tough-looking player now raised to $60. Even more surprising, the early position player made it three bets to $90. Not wanting to be bullied, Chris capped the betting at $120, and both players called. This was *his* pot, and no one was going to intimidate him! There was now $516 in the pot.

The river was the 7♥, and the early position player bet out immediately for $30. Chris, not noticing that the card actually paired the board *and* completed the flush draw, called the $30. He thought he might still have the best hand, but he was now worried about the player behind him. Sure enough, the tough guy raised to $60. The early position player now made it $90 to go. Chris was stuck. He was now certain that his hand was no good, but the pot was so big and he didn't want to appear too weak to his new opponents, so he called the extra $60. Of course, the tough guy capped the betting at $120, and both players called.

As could be expected, the early player flipped over A♥K♥ for the nut flush. And before Chris could fold his hand, the tough guy turned over Q♦Q♠ for the winning full house. No one even noticed when Chris quietly slid his cards into the muck, now too embarrassed to show his weak holding.

Chris felt sick as the pot—*his* pot—was pushed to the tough guy. He had already been counting the money in his head, thinking he'd even surprise his buddy Nolan by buying him dinner. After all, Nolan was his mentor and had taught him the ropes.

The next hand was about to start, and when Chris looked at his chips, he saw a very small stack of red $5 chips and a handful of white $1 chips. He picked them up and stumbled out of the room, still reeling from the shock. In one pot, he had lost $285—nearly his entire winnings from the $3-$6 game.

So what happened? What made Chris lose his winnings? Actually, several things happened, and we can learn from all of them.

First, Chris was playing in a game that he couldn't afford. His regular game was $3-$6, yet here he was playing in a game that could easily destroy his bankroll. $15-$30 is a long way up the ladder from $3-$6, not only in monetary values but in the quality of play. And this brings us to our second point: Chris was out-matched.

Playing over one's bankroll is dangerous, as we can see. But the danger is twofold. Playing on a small bankroll or a small buy-in is sometimes okay, but not if the players you are playing against are all better than you. Did you follow the play of the hand? Chris didn't play the hand too badly (although he did make a few mistakes, for example, defending his posted blind with a weak hand). The fact was his opponents played better than he did. Had Chris been more experienced, he might not have lost so much on the hand.

Granted, this is a fairly extreme example, but the point remains the same. Playing over one's bankroll, playing on a short buy-in, and playing against players who are well above your skill level equates to a shortcut to the ATM machine.

There are several issues related to money that we'd like to talk about in this chapter. We divide money mistakes into four main problem areas:

- Money management
- Playing scared
- Adequate buy-in
- Unreasonable expectations

Chris has trouble with the first three problem areas. And because of the horrible experience he's just gone through, he'll most likely have trouble with the last area the next time he sits down to play. We'll address these issues sequentially, allowing us to show you how to avoid the most common monetary pitfalls, and hopefully teach you a little about managing your bankroll.

Money Management

Most books on poker or gambling touch on this term. Any poker author or poker player will tell you what they think money management is, and you will receive a different answer from each one. Our definition of *money management* is basic: it's the proper building and care of your poker bankroll.

The obvious next question is, what is a bankroll? Our definition of *bankroll* is the money you use to play poker. We strongly suggest you don't spend your bankroll on travel expenses, clothing, or 52" plasma televisions. Rather, you should use it *solely* for poker. Many players go so far as to keep a separate bank account for their poker bankroll. This enables them to keep track of their money and to keep it away from normal spending money. Think of your poker bankroll as a tool of the trade. Just as a chisel is to a sculptor, so is the bankroll to the poker player. Without it, you cannot play.

Peter could have used this advice. You'll recall that Peter, although a slightly winning player, is weak-tight and a little too cautious. He's been playing low limits for a very long time, yet he never seems to build up his bankroll enough to move to the next level. After a big win at the tables (which have been rare in Peter's career due to his timid style of play), he would treat himself to a nice dinner or maybe buy a gift for his wife. Of course, that meant that his winnings weren't being re-invested in his best poker asset: himself.

Maintaining a solid bankroll is so important, yet most players who start out learning the game bypass this key aspect of success. They skip over the money management chapters in the books they read (if they read any at all), assuming that they already understand how to build and manage a bankroll. This is natural, since many players manage their own finances or even run successful businesses. Yet many of these same players go broke again and again. They either have difficulty translating these concepts from their business lives to poker, or they just don't grasp them at all.

So how big should your bankroll be? That has been a question debated among poker theorists and players alike for years. Regardless of the endless conversations, we believe that a huge majority of players are usually playing over their bankrolls—if they actually *have* a bankroll.

The casual player visiting Las Vegas or Atlantic City for the weekend usually has a certain amount of gambling money, which he refers to as "money I can afford to lose." We should all be so fortunate. These players really have no need for understanding bankroll requirements (though learning a few money-management concepts would help them), as they're gambling just for fun.

However, just by buying and reading this book, you have shown a desire to be a successful poker player. We'd like to offer some guidelines to help you build and manage your bankroll, and to assure you that you're not playing beyond the means of your current bankroll. With that in mind, the general consensus among theorists and players alike is that a player's bankroll should be *at least* 300 to 400 big bets of that player's regular game. We tend to side with the higher number. To make it easy, here are some numbers to ponder.

Limit	Suggested bankroll
$1-$2	$800
$3-$6	$2,400
$4-$8	$3,200
$5-$10	$4,000
$15-$30	$12,000
$20-$40	$16,000

These numbers might be a shock to some of you. Remember, these are *minimum requirements*. We feel more comfortable with a bankroll of 500 big bets. This does not mean that you should bring your entire bankroll to the casino with you. You only need two to three buy-ins for the game you'll be playing.

In his excellent work *Poker Essays*, Mason Malmuth goes even further with discussions on bankroll considerations. He believes (and we agree) that the higher your win rate, the lower your bankroll requirements.[24] Malmuth believes that bankroll determinations can be derived from a mathematical formula based on your standard deviation and your win rate.[25]

For no-limit hold'em players, we recommend a bankroll of no less than 20 buy-ins. For example, if your regular game is the $2/$5 no-limit hold'em at Bellagio in Las Vegas, your bankroll should be at least $4,000 ($200 × 20).[26]

For tournament players, your bankroll will vary widely depending upon your average buy-in. Because of the nature of tournament poker, the variance is very high. All this means is that, since your usual result in a tournament is a loss of your buy-in and entry fee, you will need to rely on those few times that you cash. Let's assume that you cash 10% of the time, and that your average cash in a tournament is nine times the buy-in. Let's also assume that your average buy-in to a tournament is $50. In one hundred tournaments, you'll lose $50 ninety times (-$4,500) and you'll make $450 ten times ($4,500). You're a break-even player (which is better than most). However, this does not mean that you're going to cash in one of every ten tournaments you play in. You might go twenty or even thirty (or more) tournaments before you cash. For you, we recommend a bankroll equal to fifty times the amount of your average buy-in ($2,500 in our example).

Simply stated, your bankroll needs to be large enough to handle the *variance* (up and down swings) of playing poker. There will be days when it seems like you cannot win regardless of your starting

---

[24]See *Poker Essays*, pages 59-64.

[25]For the mathematically inclined, the formula is $BR = \dfrac{9\sigma^2}{4(WR)}$ where BR is bankroll, is standard deviation and WR is win rate. See *Poker Essays*, page 59.

[26]$200 is the minimum (and maximum) buy-in in this game.

cards or the manner in which you play them. And, of course, there will be sessions where everything you touch turns to gold. That is the nature of gambling, and poker is no exception. Be prepared for fluctuations of one hundred big bets or greater (yes, we have had sessions like this several times in our playing careers, both to the good and the bad).

With an adequate bankroll, these fluctuations are much easier to handle psychologically. If you're not worried about losing half of your bankroll in a single session, you'll make better decisions at the table. This leads us into the second area of money mistakes: playing scared.

Playing Scared

Playing scared means that you are making incorrect decisions (usually on the extremely conservative side) at the table based on your current bankroll or table stake situation. Here's an example.

Justin is a loose player who plays too many hands, but he doesn't usually continue after the flop unless he has a hand. He's not a calling station, although he does sometimes go to the river with sub-par hands. He doesn't like to chase draws. He has an understanding of odds, but he doesn't always follow the play he knows to be correct. For these reasons, he is a losing player.

In his usual $5-$10 limit hold'em game, Justin has been on a steady losing run lately. He's lost over half of his bankroll in two weeks, and it seems like no matter what two cards he's dealt, he can't win. He wasn't even excited when he picked up Q♥Q♠ in late position one afternoon shortly after he'd begun playing. Mick, an aggressive player Justin had played against many times, had raised to $10 from early position. Justin called the $10, as did Peter, a weak/tight player in the big blind, who had to only call $5 more. There was $29 in the pot after the $3 rake.

The flop was K♥Q♣4♥, and as expected, Mick bet out for $5. Justin, with his two queens, raised to $10 (as he should). Peter called the two bets after thinking for a moment, and Mick re-raised to $15. Justin, remembering all the times he'd flopped a set and lost, decided to just call. Peter called too, and, going to the turn, there was $73 in the pot ($1 additional was dropped for the rake).

The turn was the 2♣. Mick bet $10, and Justin and Peter called. There was now $103 in the pot.

The river brought the 9♦ (a harmless card, in Justin's view). Mick bet the river as expected, and Justin called. But to Justin's surprise, Peter now raised. Mick looked at Peter, then at the board, then at the pot. He shrugged his shoulders and tossed in another $10 for the call. Justin also called, and he wasn't at all surprised to see Peter's J♠T♦ win the $163 pot with a straight.

"Yep, rivered again," Justin said as he tabled his set of queens. Mick tossed his cards toward the muck, but as he did, they were flipped up revealing K♣8♦.

Could Justin have won the hand? Of course, but he let his fear of losing get in the way. His recent losses had caused him to play timidly, very much unlike the aggressive style he knows to be correct. Had he re-raised a known aggressive player before the flop, there's a good chance Peter wouldn't have even been in the hand. He also should have made it four bets on the flop with his set, but he was afraid he might be up against a bigger hand (KK). He played the hand poorly and he paid for it. He had two chances to knock Peter out of the hand and he failed to capitalize on either of them.

Justin played scared. When you're making decisions at the table based on your current financial state and not on your cards, opponents, and pot odds, you're going to lose a lot of money. Justin was playing a weak style of poker because he was terrified of continuing his losing streak. He knew the correct way to play, yet he chose not to follow it. His weakened bankroll clouded his logic. Understanding and avoiding this behavior is not difficult once you are aware of it, but beware, there is another trap lurking that can cause the exact same mistakes to be made out of fear: playing with an inadequate buy-in.

Small Buy-in

Rather than give another example of a player playing scared, let's discuss buy-ins for a moment. Your *buy-in* is the amount of money you buy in for when you sit down in a poker game. These buy-in amounts will vary greatly from player to player, with most players buying in for an amount that is too small.

Too small, for purposes of this discussion, equates to an amount that puts you out of your comfort level. Would you be comfortable playing in a $15-$30 game with a $100 buy-in? Of course not, yet people take shots all the time at bigger games, and they almost always sit down with an inadequate amount of chips.

We see nothing wrong with taking a shot at bigger games once in a while, even if your bankroll can't support it (in the long term). But if you do decide to step it up on occasion, make sure you have enough money to give yourself a chance to win.

As a general guideline, we suggest starting with a table stake of no less than twenty-five big bets (25 times the big bet in a structured limit game). You should also have at least that much in your pocket should you need to buy-in for more if you start losing. Here are some numbers to consider.

Limit	Minimum Buy-In	Our Suggested Buy-In
$3-$6	$150	$200
$4-$8	$200	$200-$300
$5-$10	$250	$300-$500
$10-$20	$500	$500-$700
$15-$30	$750	$800-$1,000

Notice that even though we recommend 25 big bets, we are a lot more comfortable with a larger buy-in. We have several reasons for this.

First, a large buy-in has a positive psychological effect on your game. When you have a lot of chips in front of you, you are more likely to play an aggressive style of poker. With just a few chips, it's hard to be aggressive. Getting down to the felt is embarrassing to most players; so most players avoid doing things that can cause themselves to be short-stacked. However, a large buy-in can prevent that problem before you even start playing.

Second, a large stack of chips will often intimidate new players in the game. Imagine you're sitting at a $4-$8 hold-em game. Many players will buy into this game for $100 (sometimes less). But not you. Let's say you've bought in for $300 and have been playing for a while, you've won a couple pots, and have built your stack up to around $400. There are two other players at your table who have won a lot more than you over the course of an hour, but since you bought in for three times as much as they did, you have a much bigger stack of chips. When a new player sits down, he will invariably scan the table and see who has what. Poker players, especially those driven by ego, are very much aware of how much money a player has in front of him. It's how you keep score in poker, and it means more than you might think.

When this new player sits down and sees your huge stack of chips, he will generally react in one of two ways, both of which are good for you. He'll either avoid you, thus respecting your raises and allowing you to steal more, or he'll decide you are his target and come after you. When he does this, you can easily set him up for a trap. He's gunning for you, and he's going to give you plenty of action, which means your big hands will get paid off more frequently.

Also important is having enough chips to avoid going to your wallet. Again, it is a psychological let down to take that long walk to the cashier's cage to re-load a depleted (or destroyed) stack of chips. It's no fun to lose a hand, and then, in front of your combatants, dejectedly reach into your back pocket for your wallet and ask the dealer for more chips. Take care of that first by buying in for a larger amount.

One last thing before we leave this topic. *Don't let your stack become too small.* This is a very common error, and if you watch carefully, you'll see it all the time. For example, one of your opponents at your $5-$10 table has been losing steadily. After a particularly large pot that he saw pushed to another player, he's left with five $5 chips in front of him. He picks up AA and the best he can do is win $50 or $75 if he faces multiple opponents. But if he had purchased more chips when his stack became short, he might have been able to make several hundred dollars from the hand. Don't let your big hands go to waste because you have no chips in front of you. Give yourself a chance to get back into the game, and keep your ammunition supply up at all times. If you don't have enough money to do this, you're playing over your head.

Unreasonable Expectations

After all of this discussion of bankrolls, you may be thinking to yourself that you don't need to heed our advice to the letter. After all, you're a wining player, certainly better than most of your inexperienced opponents! You can handle playing on a smaller bankroll or table stake. You'll just win money and take care of business.

Yeah, right.

Almost every new player to poker has unreasonable expectations. They overestimate their skills, underestimate the risks, ignore the math of poker regarding expectation and variance, and charge ahead into their poker careers like a blindfolded fighter pilot.

We recently met one young gentleman at a pizza shop. He was fond of poker, and he struck up a conversation with us. We'll call him Joe (not his real name, of course, for we'd like to spare him any embarrassment).

Joe told us that he'd been playing poker ever since he saw the *World Poker Tour* on television. He'd been playing for almost a year, and he had big plans for the future: he was "going pro."

"I've got the money all lined up. I haven't lost in a tournament in almost four months. In less than two years, I'll be able to quit my job and just play poker. Cool, huh?"

"Why do you have to wait almost two years if you have the money now?" we inquired.

"Because I'll be twenty-one then," Joe told us.

Yeah. Really cool.

"I've got almost two grand in my online account and my car is almost paid for. I'm thinking about moving to Vegas, but I don't want to get carried away too early. I think I should play a couple months to get used to it first. What do you think?"

Joe, I hope you're reading this book.

Like many new players to poker, Joe was lured by the glamour of big money and the carefree lifestyle he imagined professional poker players enjoyed. The truth is, being a professional poker player is a lot more stressful than most jobs. Sure, you can set your own hours and take as much time off as you want, but it's one of the few occupations that require you to pay to go to work. Not only that, but you could put in a 60-hour work week and lose thousands of dollars in the process. Let's look at a few numbers.

Most pros aspire to win 1 to 1.5 big bets an hour; 2 big bets an hour is pushing it, though several pros do manage this feat. Let's be on the safe side and say that a solid, disciplined professional can make 1.25 big bets an hour.

Limit	Hourly Wage
$3-$6	$7.50
$4-$8	$10.00
$5-$10	$12.50
$10-$20	$25.00
$15-$30	$37.50
$20-$40	$50.00

If you're a $5-$10 player, can you survive on $12.50 an hour? Before you answer that question, think about this. You're going to need a bankroll dedicated to poker only. If you go with our minimum recommendations, you'll have $4,000. But don't forget living expenses, like food, clothes, rent/mortgage, utilities, insurance, etc. Oh, and remember that even though you're making this money gambling, it is still taxable income. Not filing can get you into a lot of trouble. You'd better play it safe and build a bankroll of at least *twice* that if you're going to be able to weather the inevitable storms of variance.

And what if you're an online poker player? We believe that, not only do you need a larger bankroll for online play, but you also need to be aware of other considerations. For example, you can play more than one table online (some online pros play eight or more tables at once). This increases your hourly win rate, but usually results in a small decrease in expectation per table. It also adds considerable stress. If playing online is your plan, be sure to take certain precautions regarding multi-tabling, including a larger bankroll and a close monitoring of your play. As soon as you find yourself making poor decisions or missing things that you would normally spot in a single game, it might be time to reduce the number of tables you're playing.

What happens if you start out on a losing streak? What happens if you have car trouble or need new tires? What if you get sick and can't play for a week? Wouldn't it be good to have about three months of living expenses saved up as well before you even begin to play?

It's not as easy as you thought, is it, Joe? But wait, you were going to play tournament poker for a living, right? Do you realize your variance in tournament poker is, in our estimate, about *five times* that of ring game play? Still planning on being a professional tournament player with your $2,000 bankroll when you turn twenty-one?

OK, so most new players don't aspire to become professionals, that's true. But one common trait shared by most new players is unrealistic expectations. This is usually the result of fantasizing after seeing poker on television, seeing a friend or acquaintance hit it big one night, or perhaps even a big win or series of wins their first time out. It's been said that one of the worst things that can happen to a gambler on his first trip to the casino is hitting a huge jackpot. Over time, these gamblers usually give back their entire jackpot *several times over.*

When you're winning, poker is easy. Nothing can stop you. You're the best player at the table, and you have finally made it. Time to quit your job and move to Las Vegas, baby! After all, if it's been this easy for a week, you will surely continue your winning ways, right? Oh yeah, there will be bumps along the way, but you'll be winning most sessions without a care. You're a poker player now, not a gambler.

A month later you're broke and wondering what happened.

Poker is gambling. Let us repeat that in case you didn't read it correctly the first time. *Poker is gambling.* Don't ever forget that. With years of study and experience, you can take a lot of the gamble out of the game with your skills, but poker remains a form of gambling. This is true for every player, regardless of their skill level or win rate. Even the best players in the world go on losing streaks; indeed, because they play at much higher stakes, their losing streaks would make the casual player sick to his stomach.

Don't plan on making three to five big bets an hour or more for the rest of the year just because you had a great run in March. It's variance. It's your average win over the course of thousands of hours of play. Most players really don't have an understanding of how good they are until they've played *100,000 hands (about 2,200 hours) or more*. Don't look at your stats after two months and assume you are a poker expert. You're not.

It doesn't matter if you've won for the past three months and have been killing the online Sit & Go tournaments; it will come to an end eventually. The losing sessions are inevitable. You *will* have nightmarish sessions where you question everything you know or thought you knew about the game. Even worse, most players go completely broke several times before finding their place in the poker world. Ask most top-name tournament pros if they've ever gone broke, then strap in for an amazing rush of poker horror stories.

No one wins all the time, and everyone goes through bad runs. *Everyone*. The better prepared you are for these bad runs, the easier they will be to handle when they happen. If you're not expecting to make eleven big bets an hour, then you won't be disappointed at the end of the year when you've made about .5 of *one* big bet per hour. After all, this makes you a winning player, and you're ahead of ninety percent of all poker players.[27]

Understanding the money (as well as the money math) of poker is essential to your success. Don't be fooled by poker celebrities on television and in magazines. Poker is a difficult way to make money, and unless you maintain reasonable expectations of your results, you will spend much of your poker career being disappointed. Having realistic expectations is an important and often overlooked step to success.

And don't forget to prepare your wallet with the proper bankroll as well. Don't have the $4,000 you need to play $5-$10? That's fine. Grind it out at $3-$6 or even $2-$4 for a few years. By the time you build up your bankroll, you'll be a much better player and more than ready for the higher limit.[28]

---

[27]And that's a conservative estimate. We would estimate that, of the entire poker-playing population, about 5% are lifetime winners.

[28]We have seen low-limit games in which the rake is so high that the games are nearly impossible to beat in the long term. Careful attention should be paid when it comes to the rakes charged at your local casino. We'd also like to add that the rake charged at most online card rooms can be lower than in brick-and-mortar casinos.

Although the game is fun, poker is work. And if you want to become a good enough player to consistently turn a profit, poker is *hard* work. But don't worry. The more you understand about money and building and managing your bankroll, the fewer surprises await you.

Losing Because You Shouldn't be Playing

A couple of years ago at Thanksgiving, some good friends from up north joined Aaron and his family for the holiday dinner. Little did Aaron know that their son Larry had the flu, and being a kind and generous soul, he shared his misery with Aaron. Two days later, while playing $8-$16 hold'em, this hand reared its ugly head.

Aaron was on the button and looked down at T♣9♠. Nolan, a very good, aggressive player who normally plays in bigger games, raised to $16 under-the-gun. Joan, re-raised to $24 from middle position. For whatever reason, Aaron called. Both blinds folded, Nolan re-raised to $32 (capping the betting), with Joan calling. Aaron called as well, so the pot was $104 (after the $4 rake).

The flop came K♥T♦6♦. Nolan bet $8. Joan thought for a moment and called the bet. Aaron called without thinking.

When the 9♣ came on the turn, Aaron felt it was his dream card. Nolan bet $16, and Joan quickly raised to $32. Aaron quickly re-raised to $48. Nolan thought for a moment and just called. But Joan made the final raise to $64, and both Aaron and Nolan called. The pot now totaled $320.

The river was the 6♥, making the board K♥T♦6♦ / 9♣ / 6♥. Nolan bet $16, and Joan raised to $32. Aaron continued to ignore his opponents, considered only his almost certainly counterfeited two-pair, and called. Nolan re-raised to $48, and Joan gave Nolan a nasty look before calling. Aaron blindly called.

Nolan showed K♠K♦ and took down the $464 pot with his full house. Joan had Q♦J♦ for the straight. Aaron's two pair finished in a distant third place. As to the errors Aaron made, they were almost too numerous to count.

First, Aaron should have folded pre-flop. T9o is *not* a good hand to play facing two raises, especially an under-the-gun raise from a good player. And a second good player re-raised. Yes, Aaron had position, but he also held T9o and he was almost certainly trailing both players.

Although Aaron hit a small piece of the flop, it was *not* a good flop for his hand. He had middle pair with a middle kicker, but *both the king and the 10 were in the playing zone and the flop had to hit one of his opponents*. But Aaron wasn't thinking about his opponents, just his own hand (and not really thinking that much either).

The turn did give him two pair, but if another player held QJ, he now had just four outs (at most). But facing a bet and a raise Aaron *knew* he was ahead, so he re-raised. Joan told him (by capping the betting) that he was wrong, but he wasn't listening.

Of course, when the board paired on the river and Nolan bet right into an opponent who had been raising, Aaron should have folded. Nolan was showing a lot of strength. Joan re-raised, and again Aaron should have folded. In any event, the errors Aaron made during the play of this hand were many.

But the most important error Aaron made wasn't in the hand. In fact, his biggest mistake took place before he even sat at the table: he went to the casino.

That morning, Aaron woke up feeling nauseous. Aaron was fighting off something (he didn't find out until that evening that his whole family got the flu, thanks to Typhoid Larry), and playing poker when you're sick is like boxing with one hand tied behind your back. Yet when you go to the casino, don't you see many people coughing, sneezing, or generally just not looking healthy?

In this chapter we look at physical issues that impact play: sickness, sleepiness, and spirits. We then take a look at psychological issues that can negatively impact your game. Finally, we examine playing in too many games online at the same time. These factors cost players huge sums of money every day.

There's a simple rule—if you're sick, sleepy, or partaking in alcohol, don't gamble. Don't play poker. In all of these cases, it's almost impossible for you to play your best game.

When you're sick, your body craves rest. Even when you have a non-contagious illness, your doctor may prescribe bed rest. Do yourself a favor and *listen to your body*. Watch television, read a book, catch up on some sleep—anything that will help your body rejuvenate. If your body isn't in good health, your mind will also suffer. Trust us, you will save money by taking time off from playing.

On the subject of alcohol, there's almost no debate. Numerous studies show that alcohol can impair cognitive ability.[29] If you use a stronger drug, the impact can be even worse. We're not going to lecture you on drugs and alcohol, but we strongly advise you to skip those when you're going to play poker. If you need to have a "drink" to fit in, we suggest ginger ale, Seven-Up, or club soda—drinks that *look* alcoholic but aren't.

Sleepiness impacts you in the same way that alcohol can: you lose your ability to think.[30] Again, there's a simple solution—go home when you begin to feel tired. You *will* save money by not playing when you're tired. Additionally, if you have to drive home, you'll be awake during your drive (and the other drivers on the road will appreciate that).

But you knew all that. We all do. Yet when we go to cardrooms and casinos, or even watch some of our friends playing online, they'll

---

[29]See, for example, the Center for Disease Control's webpage at http://www.cdc.gov/alcohol/faqs.htm; and "The Effects of Alcohol and Other Drugs," Motorcycle Safety Foundation, Irvine, CA, 1991.

[30]Balkin, T., G. Belenky, J. Leu, D.M. Penetar, K. Popp, D. Redmond, H. Sing, M. Thomas, D. Thorne, and N. Wesensten. "The Effects of Sleep Deprivation on Performance During Continuous Combat Operations." *Food Components to Enhance Performance.* Washington, DC: National Academy Press, 1994, pp. 127-135. This book is available online at http://www.nap.edu/books/030905088X/html/. See also Arnedt, J.T., A.W. MacLean, P.W. Munt, and G.L.S. Milde. "How do Prolonged Wakefulness and Alcohol Compare in the Decrements They Produce on a Simulated Driving Task?" *Accident Analysis and Prevention,* (2001), 33:337-344. See also, Dawson, D. and K. Reid. "Fatigue, Alcohol and Performance Impairment." *Nature,* (1997), 388: 235.

be drinking beers and playing for hour after hour when they're dead tired. Changing this one behavior can save you *a lot* of money.

Yet there's another factor that most players ignore: their psychological health. Almost everyone knows that *tilt* (psychological imbalance, usually related to losing a hand or series of hands) can cause players to perform poorly. Tilt that is unrelated to poker can have the same impact. Suppose you get some bad news—say you're job is going to be moved to Ohio. You're very upset, and want to take your mind off the problem. So you go to your local poker room for a few hours of "relaxation."

You may relax, but unless you get incredibly lucky your wallet will be lighter when you leave than when you walked in. If you're upset or angry, you will not play your best. Your psychological well-being is shaken. For many, a bad day will equate to a negative attitude about everything. When you start to think that everything that can go wrong will go wrong, playing poker might not be the best idea. If you're trying to escape from life's problems, you may be thinking even on a subconscious level that you'll lose to that three outer. You've entered the world of the self-fulfilling prophecy.

A self-fulfilling prophecy is when the very thought an event occurring (losing a big hand in a poker game, for example) makes it more likely to occur. Scientific studies have shown the validity of self-fulfilling prophecies;[31] indeed, these studies may have been *underestimating* their impact.[32] You can't control many of the bad events that will happen, but you *can* avoid potentially destructive actions after a bad event by avoiding gambling.

Self-fulfilling prophecies can also be made to work *for* you. Consider self-help books such as Napoleon Hill's *Think and Grow Rich*.[33] Having a positive attitude is essential to succeed in any en-

---

[31]See, for example, E.E. Jones, *Interpersonal Perception*, New York: W.H. Freeman, 1990; O. Klein & Snyder, M., "Stereotypes and Behavioral Confirmation: From Interpersonal to Intergroup Perspectives." In M.P. Zanna (Ed.), *Advances in Experimental Social Psychology* (35: 135-234), San Diego: Academic Press, 2003; and R. Rosenthal & Jacobson, L, "Teacher Expectations for the Disadvantaged," *Scientific American*, 218:19-23, 1968.

[32]S. Madon, Guyll, M, Spoth, R.L., & Willard, J., "Self-Fulfilling Prophecies: The Synergistic Accumulation of Parents' Beliefs on Children's Drinking Behavior," *Psychological Science*, 15: 837-845, 2004.

deavor. That's the case for poker, too. That's the yin side of the yin and yang of self-fulfilling prophecies.

Of course, having a positive mental attitude about the game does *not* guarantee that you will have a winning session. We've seen players go too far with a positive outlook, convincing themselves that nothing can go wrong. And that's plenty dangerous, as we can see in this hand played by Joan.

Joan was in a $1/$2 blind no-limit hold'em game. She was having a great day and felt on top of the world. She knew that she would win any hand against her nine bad opponents. Five players limped pre-flop, the small blind folded, and Joan peered down at 8♥4♠ in the big blind and checked her option.

The flop came K♠8♣3♣, giving Joan middle pair. Joan bet $10 (the pot size), and was called only by Chris. The pot was now $30. The turn was the J♥. Joan bet $25, and was again called by Chris. The pot had now ballooned to $80.

The river was the 2♥, making the board K♠8♣3♣ / J♥ / 2♥. Joan assumed that her opponent had a busted flush draw (which is what she *felt* Chris held). She wondered what bet Chris would call on the river (they both had deep chip stacks), and elected to overbet the pot, putting in $100. Chris hesitated for a moment and then called the bet.

Joan triumphantly turned over her middle pair, knowing that it would win. She noticed that the pot was *not* being pushed to her; rather, Chris was scooping up the $280 pot. She saw Chris's cards, J♣2♣, and realized that Chris had stayed in the hand with a measly flush draw. Of course, Chris started with a flush draw, turned a pair of jacks, and rivered two pair.

Joan should have been wary when Chris called her bet on the flop. After all, Joan only had middle pair and Chris could easily hold a king. When she bet the turn and Chris continued to call, she should have considered the possibility that she was behind. Her overbet on the river was a clear mistake given that she only held middle pair. She was overconfident on the river, a victim of her huge ego.

---

[33]Napoleon Hill, *Think and Grow Rich*. New York: Fawcett Crest Books, 1960 (original copyright 1937).

But having a big ego is much more of a help at the poker table than a hindrance. You may have noticed that many of poker's best players have very large egos, including Phil Hellmuth and Mike Matusow. Indeed, there have been scientific studies showing that perceived ability influences outcome in sport-related activities (and poker is definitely a sport).[34] So maintain that big ego, but don't get *too* overconfident at the poker table.

Overconfidence leads into the last problem area of this chapter. Online poker allows you to play multiple tables at once. Suppose you're substantially beating the $3-$6 limit hold'em game at your favorite site. Well, why not play two games at the same time? After a few hours of playing two tables, you're doing very well and decide to try four tables.

You can take this to the extreme, too. We know players who play *twelve* tables at the same time (and they're playing $15-$30 limit hold'em). The players we know who do this are very good players, and they play relatively short sessions. *Yet they've told us that they know their games suffer because of their multi-tabling.*

They realize that their win rate per-table is lower than when they single-table. However, given that they maintain a reasonably high win rate when multi-tabling, their overall win rate is much higher than when they single-table—what they lose in their per-table win rate they make up for in volume. Fair warning, though, the old accountants' joke about losses applies—if you have a negative per table "win rate," you can't make it up in volume! So if your win rate falls below zero, you must reduce the number of tables you're currently playing.

Unless you like funding others' online poker bankrolls, we urge you to limit your multi-tabling. Be conservative about how many tables you can play. We play —*at most*— four tables online (and frequently just one or two). When you first start playing online, begin by playing just one table. Then *gradually* play at more tables. Watch your per-table win rates. As you increase the number of tables you play, your per-table win rate will fall. As long as your overall win rate is higher, *and you feel comfortable playing the*

---

[34]F. Cury, Biddle, S., Sarrazin, P., & Famose, J.P., "Achievement Goals and Perceived Ability Predict Investment in Learning a Sport Task," *British Journal of Educational Psychology*, 67: 293-343 (September 1997).

additional table(s), you're fine. You will reach a point where either your overall win rate will be lower, or you're uncomfortable. Cut back. There's nothing wrong with playing fewer tables and making more money.

Additionally, because online poker is a faster game, players tend to play in smaller games online. A player who normally plays in $5-$10 or $8-$16 limit hold'em games might play in $2-$4 or $3-$6 games online.

As you move up in limits online, don't start by multi-tabling. Just as in brick and mortar cardrooms, the players generally are better in the higher limits. Start by playing one table, and *gradually* begin to multi-table.

If you're going to multi-table online, you should use *PokerTracker* or similar software (we have more information on *PokerTracker* in Appendix B). Using *PokerTracker* gives you the ability to learn what hands are winners for you and, conversely, what hands are costing you the most money. You will even collect data on the opponents you have faced. The successful multi-tablers we know wouldn't multi-table without using this or similar software.

Additionally, when you multi-table you have to play in a much more robotic way. It's a lot tougher to multi-table when you're playing no-limit hold'em as opposed to limit hold'em because one additional bet can be for your whole stack. A mistake in limit hold'em is just one bet. Successful multi-tablers play quite tight and usually in a straightforward way. *They make their money from the mistakes of their opponents, not their own brilliant plays.*

Indeed, successful multi-tablers ruthlessly engage in table selection (see Chapter 16, *Losing Because You Don't Use Game Selection*, beginning on page 138 for more about this). If a table turns bad, they leave. The major online sites have so many tables going that a better game is just a click away.

We'll close this chapter with an example of a not-so-successful multi-tabler. Justin was on his favorite online poker site, playing four tables of $5-$10 limit hold'em when this hand came up (on one of his four tables). He held J♣T♣ in the cutoff seat at table *zzz*. Jonas23 raised in early position. Justin couldn't recall whether he had ever faced Jonas23 before. As he contemplated his action, he saw the familiar message, "You have actions at Table *xyz*." He looked at that table on his monitor, and saw that he had 72o at that table and folded. He went back to table *zzz* and decided to click the "call any" box. He then looked at the other two tables he was on, table *zyx* where the last hand (which he folded) was still in progress, and table *yyy* where he held 9♣9♠ in the big blind. He clicked "call any" here, too, and then went back to responding to an email from his best friend.

He was interrupted from this repartee by the message, "You have actions at Table *zzz*." He opened that window and noticed that four players were in the hand: himself, Jonas23, zzyzzx in the small blind, and 787designer in the big blind. The flop had come A♦T♦7♥, giving him middle pair. zzyzzx had checked, 787designer had bet $5, and Jonas23 called. The site now beeped at him and said, "You have 23 seconds left to act."

Middle pair, that's not unreasonable, Justin thought, so he called. He was then interrupted by, "You have actions at Table *zyx*." He clicked on that window and saw that he had 82o and folded. "You have actions at Table *yyy*." Clicking on that window disclosed that six had seen the flop of A♠K♠4♥; his pair of nines didn't look good so Justin folded them.

Justin went back to Table *zzz*. He saw that zzyzzx had made a $10 bet on the turn, 787designer had called, and Jonas23 folded. He saw that the board was A♦T♦7♥ / 8♥, so he now had middle pair with an inside straight draw. Justin clicked the "call $10" box and then went to Table *yyy* where he folded another trash hand. He took a sip of his beer as he went back to Table *zzz* to look at the river.

He was about to see the river there when his screen flipped to Table *xyz* where he was under-the-gun with 7♣7♠. He clicked the "Call $5" box and went back to Table *zzz* where the Board read, A♦T♦7♥ / 8♥ / 9♥. zzyzzx had checked and 787designer had bet $10. Wow, Justin thought, I made my straight and the diamond flush draw didn't come. Justin clicked the "Raise to $20" box, then saw zzyzzx fold, and 787designer raise it to $30. Justin wondered if 787designer had made a higher straight, so he just called. Before the screen took him back to Table *yyy* he saw that 787designer had A♥T♥ for the nut flush.

Justin made numerous errors during the play of this hand (and errors in the other hands he was playing, too). Could Justin handle four tables of $5-$10 limit hold'em, replying to an email from a friend, and drinking a beer at the same time? We'll let Justin's results speak for themselves.

Of course, *we* appreciate the drinkers out there. And those not concentrating. It's much easier for us to win money from players who aren't fully there than players who are determined, thinking, and acting prudently. We'd prefer them to continue their losing ways.

Losing Because You're Not Properly Educated

Nolan and Chris were having lunch at one of their favorite casino's coffee shop. They had just spent the morning in a loose $3-$6 hold'em game. Nolan, who usually plays in a bigger game, was helping Chris work on his game. He'd decided that sitting in Chris' game would give him the best view of Chris' play, as well as allowing him to show Chris how to play certain hands in certain situations. And now their conversation was dominated by the play of hands, as so often is the case when poker players dine together.

"I don't get it," Chris said between bites of his Reuben, "Why did you check-raise that guy on the turn? All you had was second pair, and there were three cards to a flush on the board!"

Nolan smiled and replied, "Don't you get it? Those flush cards were *exactly why* I check-raised him."

"Huh?" Chris was still baffled.

"Alright, here's what happened," Nolan said. "It was a loose game. Did you notice how many people were seeing the flop? At least five players played every hand, and sometimes as many as eight. But the really good part was that it was a passive game. How often did you see a pre-flop raise? Hardly ever, right?"

Chris pondered this for a moment while he buttered his third roll. "Yeah, ok, you're right about that. But what about the hand we're talking about? There were only three players in it when you raised. That's not so loose."

"Very true. That's why the play worked. With only me and those two other guys in the hand, I was able to make a move. The guy on the button was always betting, and I knew I could chase out the other guy with some aggression. I just had second pair, like you said, but I thought I might have the player on the button beat. And so I checked the turn with the intention of check-raising if the middle player checked as well. And that's what happened."

"When the middle player checked, I figured he was pretty weak. He was not a creative player. He bet when he had it and checked when he didn't. Now the guy on the button always bet when he sensed weakness. I figured he would bet, and I could chase the other guy out with a check-raise. And if the flush card came, which it did, I might even be able to win the pot right there."

"Yeah, and that's what happened. I was really surprised when that guy folded. I thought for sure you were beat."

"I was pretty sure I was good anyway. That guy played every hand and he loved to bet, but when he thought someone was strong, he would usually fold."

"Man," Chris sighed. "There's so much I have to learn!"

"You will. It just takes time. Stick with me, kid!"

Chris did stick with Nolan, and because he was attentive and eager to learn, he became a better player. Not only was Nolan a good friend, he was also a poker mentor. Nolan had been playing poker for years before Chris met him, and because of his experience, he was able to save Chris time and money by teaching him a lot of what he'd learned.

And that's what this chapter is about: being educated. Playing poker is fun, but playing poker correctly can be a lot of work. Every winning player you see has gone through his or her own poker education. Through countless hours at the table, studying players, reading poker books, and going over hands they've played, dedicated poker players have learned to improve their games.

Players have realized over the years that study away from the table is just as important as study at the table. As recently as twenty years ago, poker players didn't have hundreds of different books on the game to study. They had to learn by putting in hours at the table. But before the age of formal poker education (there are even "poker schools" you can now attend on the Internet), players who wanted to become better developed some practices to help them do so.

One of those practices, as Chris discovered, was to obtain a poker mentor or coach. Having someone to help you in the learning process is more valuable than any book could ever be. An experienced player who is willing to share his or her knowledge will help your game in countless ways.

One of the areas all poker players need to excel at is the mental game of poker. Although it is primarily a skill game, poker is still gambling. And with every form of gambling comes variance. Handling the highs and the lows of your poker career is possibly the one thing that will make or break you. An experienced player has been through it all. There is no bad beat he's not suffered countless times himself, and there's no horrible run of cards or river suckouts he's not endured.

We're not advising you to bombard your poker mentor with bad beat stories or tales of endless hands like 94s and 83o. He's heard it all before, and we're willing to bet that constant complaining would be a sure-fire way to lose your poker mentor. Just know that when you're running bad, or have suffered a horrible injustice of bad luck, he's been there and he can help you through it. You'll find that with time, it gets easier and easier to handle. And the better you handle the emotional thrill ride that poker can be, the better you will become.

Finding a poker mentor shouldn't be difficult. Hang around a poker room long enough and you'll meet all sorts of people with a wide array of poker knowledge and experience. Finding the better players isn't hard. Just look for the individual who never loses his cool, never berates other players, and is usually cashing out with several racks of chips. Perhaps you already have a friend who is capable of being your mentor, or perhaps you've already met someone who could help you with your game. Your authors have been mentors to each other for years, and we have both benefited greatly from the experience.

Of course, having a poker mentor does not absolve you from other methods of study. To really become an expert at the game, you need to do more than just play and talk. Even if you've been playing poker for years, you may find that you're not a winning player. Although you should keep records of your wins and losses to track your progress, it's not hard to tell if you're a winning player or not.

If your wallet is frequently empty when you leave the card room, that's a sign.

So now we come to the part where you really need to work: reading poker books. Now before you roll your eyes, we have some good news. You don't really need to read all that much. While it's true that almost every poker book has something to offer, you can get a much better sense of proper play by just reading a few books. And our theory is that if you can get at least two good ideas or pieces of advice from a book, it's worth the read.

We recommend purchasing a book that deals with your game of choice. No matter what your game is, from Omaha to lowball, a book has been written for you covering that game. And the book you're reading right now is full of advice we feel will help you with your game. In this book, we have tried to include most of the major mistakes players make in poker that keep them from winning, but we don't address the finer points of individual games. That reading is up to you.

The great thing about poker books is the variety. There are so many to choose from that you will have a virtual lifetime of study if you so desire. And most poker books are written in such a way that allows you to read bits and pieces at a time and still gain a great deal of knowledge. You could read only one or two other poker books (aside from this one) and be well on your way to winning at poker. Or, you might choose to read everything you can on the game and increase your poker know-how with every new book you read.

And here's a tip: you'll get the most from your poker reading by *studying* chapters rather than just reading them. That means going over a chapter several times before moving on to the next one. Repetition is a great teacher, and with poker, that old high school axiom still holds true. Read a chapter several times until you can almost recite it verbatim. That knowledge will stick with you for years to come.

In Appendix B, we provide a list of recommended reading. We believe there are many beneficial poker books out there, and culling a short list was difficult. We hope you'll benefit from reading these books as much as we have.

But before you start to think that reading books and talking to experienced players will be your saving grace in the poker world, let's backtrack a little. Remember back a few chapters when Chris sat in a bigger game and lost a ton of money? Something else happened there that might not have been apparent, and it's something we can all learn from.

Chris, high on energy and confidence after a big win in his usual game, took an unnecessary shot at a game that was too big for his bankroll and too difficult for his limited skill. He paid for it by giving away his entire profit in just one hand. But the most important thing is what happened later.

After he had calmed down and mentally recovered from his loss, he made a decision to never play in the bigger games until he built up his bankroll and became a better poker player. In short, he learned from his past mistake. And as far as we know, Chris never made that mistake again.

Learning from your mistakes is crucial in all aspects of life, but in poker, it is one of the keys to success. Certain situations come up in poker all the time. They will repeat themselves over and over throughout your poker-playing career. The best players—those who have spent countless hours at the table—have seen nearly every possible situation, and most of them, many times over.

Being able to recognize certain situations, and more importantly, knowing what to do in each one, is what makes poker look so automatic when watching an experienced player play the game. He has seen the situation so many times that he knows exactly what's going on and how to react to it. When you've reached this level of recognition, you know you've turned a corner in your never-ending poker education.

There are two ways to recognize situations and learn from your mistakes. The first one is the most difficult, but only because it is the most time consuming. Play, play, play. There is no substitute for experience, and you can only get playing experience by playing. The problem is that playing and making mistakes can be costly. As you learn to be a better poker player, you'll no doubt be making fewer mistakes, but you'll still be making them. So how do you get around some of that? We're glad you asked.

Take notes!

There is no rule prohibiting you from writing down certain situations as they happen to you at the poker table. Recording hands where you think you played incorrectly, made a few mistakes, or played brilliantly is a valuable tool. After a long session, you can easily look back on hands you've played. Playing them out in a different environment is an excellent way to see something you might have missed. And if you're still confused about what happened, talk about the hands with your poker mentor or a fellow player.

The more effort you put into studying your past hands and situations, the better prepared you'll be the next time they come up.

And if you're an Internet player, you have even more tools at your disposal. Most online poker rooms allow you to download and save hand histories for *every hand you play* on their software! Imagine being able to go back and review an entire session, hand by hand. Depending on how much work you are willing to do, you can condense months of note taking into a single file automatically. You can even review hands in which you weren't involved.

We cover hand histories in more detail in Chapter 16, *Losing Because You Don't Use Game Selection*, beginning on page 138, but for right now, just know that the technology is there for you to use. We believe reviewing hand histories is essential in learning your weak areas and learning of your past mistakes and how to avoid them. The more you study the past, the better prepared you'll be for the future.

Another method of looking at previous hands is through simulation software. There are three products available that we think every poker player should possess. Two of these products are free so there's no excuse not to get them.

The first piece of software is *Hold'em Showdown*. This freeware product, developed by professional player Steve Brecher, can be downloaded at http://www.brecware.com/Software/software.html. This software allows you to determine the exact odds of winning between two or more hold'em hands in a showdown, or all-in, situation. The software is quite useful in determining when you should have called an opponent's all-in bet.

The second software program you should obtain is *PokerStove*. Developed by Andrew Prock, *PokerStove* allows you to calculate your hand against an opponent's *range* of hands. For example, your opponent has raised from the button all-in and you're wondering whether you should call. You hold QTo, and have an idea of what your opponent's range of hands is. You input your hand and the range of hands your opponent might hold, and *PokerStove* will determine your percentage chance of winning. *PokerStove* is a free download available at http://www.pokerstove.com. *PokerStove* works solely for hold'em.

The final software program you should consider obtaining is Mike Caro's *PokerProbe*. This software allows you to run simulation analysis for many different games, including Omaha, Omaha high/low, seven-card stud, and lowball. If you specialize in a game other than Texas hold'em, *PokerProbe* is invaluable. However, the program does have some drawbacks. It's old, and works in MS-DOS. You need to specify exact hands, and it runs the hands through the river. This program is sold by ConJelCo and other poker retailers.

This was a short but important chapter. Becoming the best poker player you can be involves a lot more than just playing the game. Not only is it essential to think about the game while you're playing, it is also important to think about the game away from the table. The more effort you put into learning the game, the better you'll become and the quicker you will find success.

Working with an experienced poker player or mentor, reading books and studying hand histories are amazingly effective ways to help you improve your game that you may not have thought about before. But that's why we wrote this book: to teach you how to become a better player. We hope you will put some effort into thinking about the game away from the table, but that's up to you. How far will you go?

Losing Because You Don't Understand the Math of Poker

Math is intrinsically involved in poker. The only math skills needed for success are addition, subtraction, multiplication and division. And that really is all you need to determine pot odds, to understand variance, and to refute some basic math misunderstandings. You don't need calculus, differential equations, or a computer to be successful at the poker table. The math involved is pretty simple (see Appendix A for a brief review of pot odds and variance).

Of course, what's simple for us is not so simple for Mrs. Goldman. She was in her favorite $8-$16 game, and was in the big blind. Mick, the known maniac you may remember from previous chapters, had raised from middle position. Michelle called from the button. After the small blind folded, Mrs. Goldman peered down at her cards: Q♥Q♦. Although a raise with her queens would have been a good play, she simply called. After $4 in rake was taken, the pot stood at $48.

The flop was Q♠8♠3♣. Mrs. Goldman carefully (for her) examined the flop and realized that she had the best possible hand. So she bet $8. Mick immediately raised to $16. Michelle thought for a moment and called. Mrs. Goldman could have (and should have) reraised, but she again just called.

The turn was the 9♠. This put out a possible flush (which Mrs. Goldman noticed) and a possible straight (which she didn't notice). She decided to bet $16. Mick noticed both possibilities and decided that calling, not raising, would be a good idea. After all, every so often Mrs. Goldman picks up a real hand. Michelle liked the turn card, however, and she raised to $32.

Mrs. Goldman angrily stared at Michelle. She just knew that Michelle had made the flush. But then a light came on—she could still win the hand if the board paired. So she made the Herculean effort (for her) to count her outs.

Mrs. Goldman saw that there were three 9s, three 8s, and three 3s that could come on the river to make her hand good. Now she tried to count the number of unknown cards. Her teacher had shown her how to do this just last week, and after straining to remember how, she started with the 52 cards in the deck, subtracted the two in her hand and the four on the board, and came to 46 cards. She then figured there was a 9/46 chance of her winning the hand. She thought that was close enough to 9/45, a fraction she knew was equivalent to a one-in-five chance (or 20%). She then stared at the board and just knew that there was enough money in the pot to call. So after her two-minute trance, she called.

Mick was faced with a different problem. He had also been dealt a real hand, A♠A♣. He had worked out the math on his hand much quicker, and immediately called. (We'll examine Mick's dilemma a bit later.)

The river was the K♠, giving Mick the nut flush. Mrs. Goldman disgustingly checked. Mick, planning to check raise the river, also checked. Michelle, who did not have the flush (she actually held J♥T♥ for the straight) thought that either Mick or Mrs. Goldman had made the flush, so she also checked. Mick ended up taking down the pot.

Let's examine the math problem Mrs. Goldman faced. First, hopefully you noticed that Mrs. Goldman had ten outs, not the nine she counted. She would also have won the hand if the river had been the lone remaining queen (giving her four queens). An unlikely occurrence for sure, but it can (and does) happen. Correctly stated, Mrs. Goldman had a 10/46 chance of winning the hand, or a 21.7% chance.

Mrs. Goldman simplified her division to 9/45, or 1/5, because it was easier to do in her head. *Making fractions easier to solve is fine for poker.* Just remember the direction you simplified. In this case, the chances were slightly better than one-in-five of her making the full house (or quads).

Mrs. Goldman skipped the next step in a pot odds question: whether the money in the pot justified her action. She just looked at the pot and figured there was enough money in there. While this is *usually* the case in limit hold'em, it is usually *not* the case in no-limit hold'em. Of course, to correctly answer this question you must know how much money is in the pot. And frankly, that skill is beyond Mrs. Goldman's ability.

There was $48 in the pot pre-flop. On the flop, three players each put $16 in the pot (a bet and a raise), so there was $96 in the pot before the turn. When Mrs. Goldman faced the raise, she and Mick had put in $16 while Michelle had put in $32. Mrs. Goldman could have reasoned that Mick would likely call, and she would have to put in $16 (Michelle's raise) to win $188 ($96 [through the flop] + $64 [already bet on the turn] + $16 × 2 = $32 [her call and Mick's call]). She would then compare the ratio of the money she'd bet to the money she could win (here, $16/$188 = 8.5%) to her chance of making her hand (21.7%) and if the chance of making her hand was higher, she would call. Thus, Mrs. Goldman got it right when she called.

For Mick, though, the call was much more problematic. Mick knew that Michelle *could* have the flush (which she didn't hold) *or* the straight (which she did hold). This is a much tougher hand for Mick because if Michelle had the flush, two of Mick's outs were gone. Mick had either eight outs (if Michelle had the straight) or six outs (if Michelle had the flush). Mick did the math for his worst-case scenario, 6/46, giving him a 13.0% chance of winning. Given that this percentage was higher than 8.5%, he correctly called.

Of all poker games, hold'em is the easiest in which to determine the odds. There are only a few numbers you need to know:

- 52 – The number of cards in the deck;
- 13 – The number of cards in each suit;
- 4 – The number of cards in each rank *and* the number of cards in a one-way straight draw; and
- 2 – The number of cards in each hand.

That's it. Just four different numbers allow you to do all the calculations you need to calculate pot odds. If even Mrs. Goldman can get it nearly right, you can too.

Of course, we have to work these odds. Let's look at some normal draws you might hold (or face). If you have an open-ended straight draw, you have $2 \times 4 = 8$ outs. If you hold two suited cards, and the flop contains two of your suit, you have $13 - 2 - 2 = 9$ outs. The table below presents the number of outs you have for some common draws and your chance of making the draw with both two cards (the turn) and one card (the river) to come.

Draw	Number of Outs	Chance With Two Cards to Come	Chance With One Card to Come
Flush	9	35.0%	19.6%
Open-Ended Straight	8	31.5%	17.4%
Gutshot Straight	4	16.4%	8.7%
Straight *and* Flush	15	54.1%	32.6%
Open-Ended Straight Flush (chance of making *just* the straight flush)	2	8.4%	4.3%

Complex cases are fairly easy to work out. Let's say you hold J♦T♦, and the board is Q♦9♦3♠. How many outs do you have?

You have the eight outs for the straight, and the nine outs for the flush. However, you do *not* have seventeen outs; you must subtract the two outs that are double-counted: the K♦ and 8♦ are both straight and flush outs.

Let's look at a problem that Justin, our jamming no-limit player, faced at a brand new $2/$5 blinds $500 fixed buy-in no-limit game. Justin was in the big blind, and four players had limped (the small blind folded), and Justin checked his option with 7♦4♠. After the rake, there was $26 in the pot.

The flop came K♣6♥5♦, giving Justin the straight draw. Justin figured that the king likely hit someone's hand, and given his lack of position, a check was the best course of action. After Justin's check, Chris bet $20. Joan folded, Mick called, and Jerrod folded. Justin then called. After the rake, there was $83 in the pot.

The turn was the 5♠. Justin didn't think the card was likely to help anyone. However, all he had was an out-of-position draw, so he checked. Chris quickly checked, but Mick bet $20 into the pot. Justin had calculated that he had eight outs, and with 46 unknown cards, he had a 17.4% chance of making his hand. He had to call $20 to win $103, so he was just short of the proper pot odds to make the call.

However, Justin knew about *implied pot odds*. Justin realized that it was quite likely that if he called and made his hand on the river, he could get all (or at least a large part of) Mick's stack. Justin felt that these implied odds gave him the correct price to call Mick's bet.

But Justin had gone a step further in his thinking. Rather than calling, why not raise on a semi-bluff? After all, he was in one of the blinds, and he could easily have a hand like 65, which would give him a full house, or just a 5 for trips. And if he made a large enough bet, he wouldn't be giving Mick the odds to call for his draw. Justin also loved making large raises and intimidating his opponents, so he elected to raise to a total of $200.

Mick looked ill as he saw Justin raise. However, before he acted he noticed Chris calmly making the call. Mick immediately realized that his A♦K♦ wasn't good, as at least one of his opponents had flopped a set. Mick folded. The pot was $503 heading to the river.

Justin was delighted to see the 8♥ on the river, making his straight. Justin realized that if he bet all of his remaining chips ($275), it was unlikely that Chris would call. He decided that Chris would call a bet of $150 if he had hit something, and that's what he bet. Chris looked at the board, checked his hole cards, and calmly said, "I'm all-in." Justin didn't bother to think about it; instead, he quickly said, "Gotcha! I've got the nut straight. I call!" As Justin was eyeing the $1,053 pot, he was startled to see Chris's hand: 5♣5♥, giving Chris quad fives. Justin began grumbling about his "bad beat."

Of course it was anything but a bad beat as Chris was ahead of Justin the entire hand. Pot odds are useful, but Justin had the experience of drawing dead and getting there. Poker isn't played in a vacuum. Even on a pot odds problem, you *must* consider what your opponents hold. Justin's play on the flop was fine. His semi-bluff raise on the turn was an aggressive but reasonable play. However, when he's called by Chris, who bet the flop but checked the turn, he should have given more thought to what Chris might hold. Mick asked himself this question and believed that either Chris or Justin flopped a set. Justin should have realized that Chris had a very strong hand; this would have saved him at least part of his stack on the river.

You may have noticed another error that Justin made. He held the second best straight. The top straight (97) was yet another potential hand that Chris could hold that would beat Justin's hand.

A common problem that all poker players face is separating perception from reality. We act based on our perceptions of facts, not the facts themselves. This includes our memory of bad beats. We remember when our opponents hit their one or two outers to take down a huge pot that should have been ours, but do we recall the numerous times when our opponents *don't* get the necessary river card and we win the large pot?

These "good beats" aren't memorable because they're normal. The human brain processes so much information that normal events are not catalogued. Do you remember what clothes you wore three months ago? Unless that date was a memorable occasion for you (for example, an anniversary), you probably have no recollection of what you wore that day.

Another time this occurs at the poker table is with one-suited flops. We all recall the times when we've had a big pair, the flop comes one-suited—and, of course, we don't hold the overcard of that suit. Consider what happened to our multi-tabling Internet player, Justin.

Justin was playing in two $3-$6 limit hold'em games at his favorite online card room. To his surprise and delight, he was dealt K♥K♦ at both tables at the same time. Needless to say, Justin fired out a raise in each game, and three players called him at each table, including the blinds.

At the first table, the flop came K♣4♦4♥, giving him a full house. Justin bet the flop and was called by Joan in the big blind. The turn was the 2♥. Joan checked, Justin bet, and Joan raised. Justin reraised and Joan called. The river was the 9♦. Joan checked, Justin bet, and Joan called. Justin's full house beat Joan's smaller full house (4♣2♣), and Justin took down the $75 pot (after the $3 in rake).

At the other table, the flop was Q♣T♣9♣. It was again checked to Justin, who bet the flop. Only Jerrod, in the big blind, called. The turn was the 2♥. Jerrod checked, Justin bet, and Jerrod called. The river was the 3♣. Jerrod bet the river, and Justin reluctantly called. Jerrod turned over K♣Q♠, and his flush took down the $52 pot (after the $2 in rake).

Exactly one orbit later at Jerrod's table, Justin again picked up a big hand: A♠A♣. Justin raised, and three players called him, including both blinds. The flop was annoying to Justin, another one-suited monstrosity: Q♥7♥3♥. It was checked to Justin, and he knew that no matter what happened, he was doomed to lose the hand, so he also checked. The turn was the 2♣. Again, everyone checked. The river was the 6♦. Jerrod, in the big blind, bet. Justin was the only caller. Jerrod had 6♣2♠ for two pair and took the pot.

Later that day Justin was talking with his friend Chris about his online session. Did Justin bring up the big pot he took down when he flopped a full house? Of course not. Did he talk about the other big hands he won during his session? No. Instead, he brought up the two one-suited flop hands that he had lost.

There wasn't anything Justin could do about the first hand he lost. He correctly bet every street, but Jerrod had the right price to call for his draw. Jerrod got lucky (and Justin unlucky) on the river when he hit the club for the flush.

On the second hand, Justin got gun-shy. He *knew* he would lose the hand, and he created a situation where he lost a hand he should have won. Had he bet the flop or the turn, he would have taken down the pot. (It's unlikely Jerrod would have called with his pair of deuces on the turn.) But by fearing the flush, he created the situation where Jerrod's inferior hand became the best hand at the river.

If you have two suited cards, what are the odds of flopping a flush? There are eleven cards in your suit outstanding, so the chances of flopping a flush are:

$$Flush\ Chance = 11/50 \times 10/49 \times 9/48 = 0.84\%$$

That's right, you will flop a flush *less than one percent of the time*! The odds against this happening are about 118 to 1. You will flop a flush *draw* an additional 10.9% of the time. Players fear one-suited flops in hold'em, but most of the time the flush won't be outstanding.

Another reason why some players remember one-suited flops is due to the nature of online poker. Internet players see many more hands per hour, and can play more than one table at a time. Because they see so many hands, they will see more bad beats and memorable hands. These hands stick in the mind and lead to the popular conspiracy theories about online poker games being rigged.

We don't believe that these games are rigged. Forgetting the fact that it's not in the best interests of any Internet site to have a rigged game, the statistics behind bad beats and memorable hands guarantee that online players *will* see some in a session. Let's assume that on one particular hand there's a 5% chance of a bad beat happening. If this happens five times during your session, what is the chance of you observing such a bad beat? It's 22.6% $(1 - 0.95^5)$. If ten such situations happen, your chance of observing a bad beat is 40.1% $(1 - 0.95^{10})$.[35] Thus, Internet players see lots of memorable hands because they see so many hands being played.

We've diverged a bit from pure mathematics in this chapter. The math that's needed to be successful at the poker table isn't that difficult. Most of the time, you will know what to do regardless of the math involved. When a pot odds problem does occur, calculate the odds and act with them. You may win or lose the hand, but if you go with the odds over time you *will* be a winner.

---

[35]To compute the odds of a bad beat happening, you calculate the chance of it *not* happening, and then subtract this from 1 (the chance of an event happening or not happening must equal 100% = 1). In the first example, we have five events, each with a 5% chance of a bad beat. The chance of a bad beat not happening in each case is 95%. The chance of *no* bad beat occurring is 0.95 $\times 0.95 \times 0.95 \times 0.95 \times 0.95 = 0.95^5$. The chance of a bad beat *occurring* must equal 1 – the chance of no bad beat = 1 - $0.95^5 = 0.226 = 22.6\%$. In the second example, similar reasoning gives the chance of no bad beat as 0.95^{10} and the chance of a bad beat as 1 - $0.95^{10} = 40.1\%$.

FOURTEEN

Losing Because You're Playing in Tournaments

You look down at your cards, J♣J♥, and realize that you've trapped your world-class opponent and are just moments away from winning the main event of the *World Series of Poker*. Holding A♠T♠, your opponent must catch an ace, and he's drawing very slim with the board of 5♣3♦K♦ / 7♠. You're standing and waiting. Finally, the dealer burns, and is about to reveal the river when…the alarm on your radio wakes you up.

We've all daydreamed about winning the *World Series of Poker* main event. With thousands of entrants, a first place prize in the millions, and "no-name" players winning in the last few years, why wouldn't you daydream about this? After all, if John Noname can be the world champion, why can't you or I?

If only it were that easy. In this chapter we will explore the math behind tournaments, and the huge (and we mean *really huge*) variance that exists in today's uber-large fields. And the conclusion we draw will seem hard to believe too many of you. Tournaments are *not* a good buy for the average player.

Many of you probably became interested in poker because you saw the *World Poker Tour* or the *World Series of Poker* on television. Tournaments are exciting, and no-limit hold'em makes excellent drama (and, thus, excellent television). But have you noticed the number of *races* (where two players have fairly equal hands, such as a pair versus two overcards) that happen? In order to win a tournament, players must win these coin-flip hands. The luck factor in tournaments is huge.

Of course, that doesn't mean you shouldn't play tournaments. Let's examine the math behind a tournament. Assume that exactly 100 players enter a tournament, and that the top ten players make the money. We'll assume that the cardroom charges $125 per person for entry into this tournament; of this, $100 goes into the prize pool and $25 is kept by the cardroom (the *juice* or *vig*).

Assume further that this tournament is run twice a week, and you enter it every time it's offered for fifty weeks, so that you play in it 100 times. You're an average player, and you finish in every possible place once. Thus, after the 100 entries you're out the fee charged by the cardroom, $25 × 100 = $2,500.

We can see that the average player gets $100 back per week. In order to *just break even,* you must earn $125 per tournament. In order to be a winning player, you must exceed this figure. Given that the *average* is a $25 loss per tournament (net), it's clear that there are fewer winners than there are losers among regular tournament players playing these tournaments.

It is true, though, that as the buy-in cost of a tournament increases, the juice charged by the casino drops. For a $200 tournament, the juice is typically $30 (15%), for a $300 tournament, it's $40 (13%), and for a $500 tournament, it's $50 (10%). At the very large buy-in tournaments such as those on the *World Poker Tour* or the *World Series of Poker,* the juice is even less when measured on a percentage basis. At the Bicycle Casino's 2005 *Legends of Poker* main event (televised by the *World Poker Tour*), the entry fee was $5150, inclusive of the $150 juice (3%). The *World Series of Poker* charges juice between 6% and 10% for every event. Additionally, most major tournaments withhold 2% to 4% of the prize pool for a mandatory "tip" or "service charge." There are additional costs when you play major tournaments; these include the cost of lodging, air travel, and meals. If you're an online tournament player, the juice charged is significantly less, and is usually 5% to 10% of the buy-in.

Since the higher buy-in tournaments have a lower juice, you might believe that they are better values. And that would be the case if the quality of players were the same at higher levels (as they are at lower levels). However, just as the players get better (in general) as you move up in levels, the players tend to be better in the higher buy-in tournaments.

Another factor against playing in tournaments is variance. Let's take a look at an end-game example of variance. Assume that you are heads-up in a tournament against the chip leader. The blinds and antes are very small compared to your chipstack. Unfortunately, you find yourself trailing the chip leader and will need to double up several times in order to pull even with him. But luck is on your side, to one extent—you are dealt A♦A♥ on *every* hand while the chip leader is dealt K♦K♥ on *every* hand. Obviously, you are the favorite on each hand. How many hands will it take, on average, for the *chip leader* to knock *you* out of the tournament? We'll look at the answer to this question in a few moments.

Variance takes many forms in tournaments. Some of these factors are the quality of players at your table, the way players play at your table, and the cards you receive. Let's take a look at these issues.

Almost all tournaments use some form of random draw for seating assignments. This means that you could be placed at a table with eight individuals playing no-limit hold'em for the first time, or conversely, eight world champions. The nature of your opponents is a factor that you cannot control, and it increases the variance inherent in tournament play.

Luckily, most of the time you will face a "typical" table for the tournament you've entered. But how do your "typical" opponents play? Assume that you're in a no-limit hold'em tournament. Will you face tight, conservative players? Will you face players who are maniacs? Will you face players who only know one move—to make all-in bets? The nature of your opposition is another factor that you can't control, and it too adds to your variance.

An additional significant factor is the nature of your cards. Yes, poker is a people game played with cards, but it's much easier to win holding good cards than it is bad cards. Additionally, in most tournaments you will face *race* or *coin-toss* situations where you hold a pair and face two overcards or vice versa. In order to win a tournament, you must win these coin-tosses. Given the obvious fifty-fifty nature of these races, you will lose them about half the time. Thus, your cards really impact your variance.

Even when you get good cards, you can lose by having a *bad beat* or a statistical anomaly. Let's look at the scenario described above where you hold two aces and face two kings. Poker is very different than games such as chess where confrontations are determined by rules. Poker, a form of gambling, has its confrontations resolved by the luck of the cards. When you hold A♦A♥ and face K♦K♥, you will lose 17.1% of the time.

We can determine when, on average, you will lose by using the laws of probability. If you have a 17.1% chance of losing the hand, you have a 1 − 17.1% = 82.9% chance of winning the hand. We multiply the chances together (82.9% × 82.9% × 82.9%...) until the probability is less than 50%. This happens after four times, meaning that, on average, you will lose an A♦A♥ versus K♦K♥ confrontation one out of four times.

So even when you get good cards, and do everything right, you can *still* lose when you get unlucky. And if it can happen to you after just four times when you hold AA, it can certainly happen when you have lesser holdings. So how does one win a tournament when you face several thousand competitors?

Yet get very lucky, of course. The winner of the main event of the *World Series of Poker* is an excellent player, but it might be more correct to call him the *luckiest* excellent player. He is the player who wins the coin flips and gets good cards when he needs them. He also plays well.

Take the 2005 *World Series of Poker* as an example. On the very first hand of the tournament, Oliver Hudson holds TT and faces Sammy Farha who holds AT. Pre-flop, Sammy Farha raises to $200, Oliver Hudson re-raises (the blinds are $25/$50) to $450, and Sammy Farha calls. The flop comes AAT—Sammy Farha flops the nut full house and Oliver Hudson flops a full house. Almost all of us would go broke if we held TT, as Oliver Hudson did. That's pure bad luck, and it can happen to anyone.[36]

The argument that we hear the most for playing in tournaments with a large field is the amount of *dead money* (money contributed to the prize pool by players with almost no chance of winning the tournament) in the field. Let's assume that the main event of the

---

[36]One can definitely argue that Oliver Hudson should have re-raised to more than $450 (and we would agree). The point of this example is to illustrate that bad luck happens in the real world, and even when you hold a hand that dominates your opponent you can lose. Pre-flop, Oliver Hudson was a 65.2% favorite over Sammy Farha.

World Series of Poker has a field of 6,000 entrants. You consider yourself an excellent player—far better than the average entrant. We'll assume that you will win the tournament three times as often as the average player. Where the average player will win once every 6,000 times, you will win once out of every 2,000 times. Unfortunately, the laws of mortality trump the laws of probability—you are *very* unlikely to win the tournament during your lifetime.

We believe this argues persuasively against spending $10,000 to enter the *World Series of Poker* main event. However, if you can win a satellite to enter the event (thus drastically decreasing your cost to enter the event), the risk-reward ratio improves dramatically.

But you want to give it a shot, try for your dream like Robert Varkonyi, Chris Moneymaker, Greg Raymer, or Joe Hachem. If you've got a spare $10,000 and don't care about your results, go for it. However, even if you're the best unknown player in the world, your most likely result is a loss of $10,000.

So how do good tournament players—and there are quite a few—overcome the inherent variance in tournaments? There are two methods: playing a lot of tournaments, and being backed. Most players on the tournament circuit do both. And every player should want to keep their variances low along with keeping their win rates high.

An excellent tournament player might consider his average result (the statistical *mean*) in a $10,000 buy-in tournament to be a win of $3,200. Of course, this comes from winning one tournament (and netting, let's assume, $1,500,000), placing in a couple of others (netting $5,000 twice), and losing a large number of other buy-ins. Indeed, his *median* result is a loss of his $10,000 entry fee. But our hypothetical tournament pro plays in most of the big buy-in tournaments, so over one year he obtains his expected result.

In statistics, the *Central Limit Theorem* specifies that if a population is large enough, it will be normally distributed (appear like a bell curve).[37] A consequence of this is that sample results will approach the expected result. Thus, the more tournaments a player enters, the more that his average sample result will approach his theoretical result.

As noted earlier, tournaments are expensive. Another method that the tournament pro uses to lower variance is the assistance of a "backer." The backed pro will sign a contract with a backer where he exchanges some percentage of his winnings for financial support from the backer. If the pro can keep the exchanged percentage low while receiving as much financial support as possible, he will lower his risk by increasing his backer's risk.

Some tournament players engage in another potentially unethical means of lowering variance. They exchange "pieces" of themselves with other pros playing in the same event. Let's say that Joe sees Jane in the event, and knows that Jane is a good player. Joe might approach Jane and ask her if she's willing to swap 5% of their results. Such trades are almost always straight swaps of small percentages (up to 5% is typical).

This effectively lowers the variance for the pro. To see this, let's assume that there is a tournament with just five entrants: four pros and one amateur. We'll assume that each pro is equally likely to win, and that the amateur is only half as likely as a pro. Each pro has a 22.2% chance to win, and the amateur has an 11.1% chance.[38] If the tournament costs $22 (with $2 going to the house), and is winner take all, each pro's expectation is to win 22¢, while the amateur's expectation is to lose $10.88.

But now assume that the pros each exchange 5% of themselves with each other. Their expected results will remain the same (given that each pro has the same chance of winning, they will each own 85% of their result, and 5% of each of the other pro's results), but their variance *must* go down. Given that the tournament pays only one place, each pro can expect to win 22.2 times for every 100 times they enter the tournament. *But they're only playing this particular tournament once.* In this tournament, they will end up with one of two results, a win (netting $78), or a loss (losing $20). If they ex-

---

[37]The theorem states, "If a simple random sample of n observations is to be taken from a population with finite mean and variance, the distribution of the sample mean $\bar{\chi}$ will approach a normal distribution as n approaches infinity. In general, if a sample is large enough, and the shape of the populations *looks* like a normal distribution, the closer the sampling distribution of $\bar{\chi}$ will approach normality.

[38]0.1% is lost due to rounding.

change with all the other pros, they're more likely to take home some money (thus lowering their variance).

There's another potential consequence of swaps and backing: not trying your hardest against players that you back. Suppose you back Jane. You both reach the final table of a major tournament. On a particular hand, you're holding T♠T♣ in the big blind and facing a raise from Jane. You read Jane as having either an AK or an underpair to your tens. Do you re-raise all-in, forcing the decision back to Jane, or do you fold, not wanting to get into a confrontation at this point?

We believe quite strongly that most backers *would* consider that they're backing Jane if this situation were to arise. Sure, tournament ethics dictate that you're not supposed to consider such an issue; however, no one but you, Jane, and the IRS (and possibly the organizers) would know about the backing relationship, so soft-playing someone you back is entirely probable. We're quite cynical about this, but until tournament poker requires that all backing and swaps be publicly announced (or posted at the playing site), we think this is a scandal that *will* erupt one day.[39]

So what does the non-tournament pro do? Should you avoid all tournaments, and just play cash (ring) games? Are there any tournaments where you can have an advantage?

There are two types of tournaments that we believe offer potential profits for non-tournament pros, Sit & Go's and non-hold'em tournaments. Almost all online sites offer Sit & Go's, nine or ten person one-table tournaments. The cost to enter these tournaments begins at $5.50 and goes up from there (the house usually keeps 10% of the entry cost, $0.50 out of the $5.50, $1 out of $11, etc.). These tournaments award prizes to the top three players, 50% of the prize pool for first place, 30% for second and 20% for third. We've found these tournaments to be good values at the lower buy-ins ($33 and under). If you're looking for a strategy guide to Sit & Go's, we strongly recommend the third edition of Lee Jones' *Winning Low-Limit Hold'em* (see Appendix B for more information). Lee has included three chapters on strategy in these mini-tournaments.

---

[39]Rule 7 of the Tournament Directors Association (TDA) rules states, "A penalty MAY be invoked...if soft-play occurs...." [Emphasis in original] This is the only mention of soft-play in the TDA rules.

We also like non-hold'em tournaments. Most poker players simply don't know how to play Omaha high/low tournaments, seven card stud tournaments, or stud high/low tournaments. Unfortunately, there just aren't many of these tournaments spread anymore. Yes, if you enter one of these you'll likely face a tournament specialist in one of these games, but we still believe that there is an opportunity to make money in non-hold'em tournaments.

Frankly, most tournaments today are *not* a good value for the average player. In fact, most pros acknowledge that if the "dead money" (the average players) didn't enter the tournaments, they would be poor values *even for the pros*. This doesn't mean that you shouldn't enter tournaments. They're a great way to learn a game with a limited (usually fixed) cost. And let's face it; they're fun! Unfortunately, the combination of relatively high costs (entry fees), large fields (making them more of a lottery than a game of skill), and the very high luck factor inherent in all tournament play persuasively argue against the average player making tournament poker his or her normal form of poker.

Losing Because Of Bad Luck

As we commented in the last chapter, you *must* be lucky to win a tournament. Luck impacts cash games, too. Consider this hand played by Peter, a tight player who tends to play like a calling station. Peter was dealt 7♣7♠ in the big blind in an $8-$16 limit hold'em game. Michelle and Chris had limped, but Joan raised from the button. Peter decided to call, figuring that Michelle and Chris would likely call from behind him. He wasn't disappointed—both Michelle and Chris called. There was $64 in the pot (4 players at $16 each, plus the $4 small blind, less $4 in rake).

The flop was exactly what Peter wanted: T♥7♦3♠. He had flopped a set, there were no likely flush or straight draws out against him, and Joan might have an overpair and be in big trouble. Peter checked the flop, deciding that a check-raise would be the best play. Michelle checked as well, but Chris decided to bet. And when Joan raised, Peter began to fear that maybe Michelle or Chris had pocket 10s, so he just called the extra bet. Michelle folded and Chris called the raise. The pot had grown to $112.

The turn was the 2♣. Peter knew that card couldn't have helped anyone, but he still feared pocket 10s. After considering his decision for nearly thirty seconds, he checked. Chris checked also, but Joan continued to show strength by betting $16. Peter and Chris called the bet. The pot was $160 heading to the river.

The river brought the J♠, making the board T♥7♦3♠ / 2♣ / J♠. Peter wondered if Chris had stayed in the hand with a straight draw, like 9♥8♥. And then his heart *really* began to ache—he just knew that Joan had pocket jacks and had rivered him. He checked. Chris, too, checked. Joan turned over her A♥K♥ and said, "Nut no-pair." Peter and Chris flipped over their hands (Chris had A♠T♠) and Peter's set won the $160 pot.

On the very next hand, Peter was in the small blind. Again, Michelle and Chris limped into the pot. Joan, now in the cutoff seat, also limped. After the button folded, Peter eyed his hole cards, A♣K♣, and he raised to $16. All of the limpers called (the big blind folded), making the pot $68 going to the flop after the rake of $4 was collected.

The flop came K♥7♦3♠, giving Peter top pair, top kicker. Peter bet, Michelle called, Chris folded, and Joan called. The pot was up to $92.

The turn was the irrelevant (to Peter) 2♥. He knew that card couldn't have helped anyone. Confidently, Peter tossed his $16 bet into the pot. He was surprised when Michelle was hesitant about her action. Was she actually considering raising? After a long hesitation, she called. Then, to Peter's surprise, Joan raised to $32. Attempting to disguise the strength of his hand, Peter only called. Michelle, after another hesitation, also called. The pot had grown to $188.

The river was the T♠, making the board K♥7♦3♠ / 2♥ / T♠. Peter decided that he would check-raise Joan and show her who the real poker player was. He checked, as did Michelle. And after Joan bet, Peter continued with his plan and check-raised to $32. But to his surprise, Michelle re-raised to $48 (after checking). Joan reluctantly called, and Peter was forced to give the hand some more thought. Michelle acted as if the deuce on the turn had helped her—could she have pocket deuces? And Joan is acting like *she* had a good hand. Peter finally thought that his hand wasn't good, but the pot was so large he just had to call. He did, and Michelle turned over her hand, exclaiming, "Finally, the Hammer is a winner," and displayed the 7♥2♣. Joan then flipped over her hand, 3♥3♦, and took down the $332 pot with her set of threes.

That evening, Peter was talking with his poker buddy Aaron, bemoaning his bad luck on these two hands. "I flop a set, but the board looks scary, so I'm forced to just check-call, and then I flop top pair, top kicker, and some donkey calls me down with %*$&#@ing seven-two offsuit!" Peter conveniently ignored the pocket threes that won that hand. "I can't believe my miserable luck," he added.

Was Peter really unlucky? He certainly thought so, but perhaps he didn't make the most of his first hand. After all, when flopping a set against a likely overpair, you stand to pick up a big pot. Should Peter have gotten more from the first hand?

Definitely. *You can't play scared!* If you do, we guarantee that your wins will be smaller than they should be, and your losing sessions will be far worse than they should be. Let's examine the first hand in depth.

Peter got his dream flop, hitting a set. Given that there were probably no flush or straight draws out against him, check-raising on either the flop or turn would have been a good play. And indeed, that was his strategy. Yet when Chris bet, he instantly decided that his second-nut hand was beaten. So he deviated from his plan and just called. This would still be reasonable *if* he raised on the turn.

Peter made two mistakes on the turn. First, he noticeably hesitated. If you make all your bets at the same tempo, your opponents cannot get a read on your hand from the speed in which you bet. Mae West put it well, "He who hesitates is a damned fool." Second, Peter still feared the absolute nuts being out against him. He should have check-raised; this would have increased the pot by $48 and his winnings by $32.

On the river, Peter continued to play scared poker. He should have followed up the check-raise on the turn with a bet on the river. Had he done so, it's likely that only Chris would have called (with his pair of tens); still, that would have been an additional $16 on the river that he could have (and should have) won. All told, Peter should have won an additional $48 on this hand.

Also notice Joan's betting. Joan represented an overpair throughout the hand by raising on the flop and betting the turn. She had the guts to continue taking shots at the pot with nothing. When both of her opponents called on the turn, she knew that a third bluff on the river would not succeed; at least one of her opponents had a made hand.

Now let's examine the second hand from Joan's viewpoint. Joan elected to limp into the pot with pocket threes, hoping to flop a set. Like Peter on the first hand, she got lucky and did flop the set. She decided that a raise on the turn would be a winning action. And unlike Peter, Joan followed through on the raise even though it was possible that Peter raised with pocket kings. Joan rightly discounted the possibility that Peter had flopped a higher set. Indeed, when an opponent flops a higher set you usually must smile and take your loss.

Let's assume that Peter would raise in the small blind with AA, KK, QQ, JJ, TT, or AK. Let's further assume that Peter, being a weak-tight player, would *not* have bet the flop had an overpair come. Thus, we can limit his hands to AA, KK, or AK. There are six ways of being dealt AA. With one king outstanding, there are only three ways of being dealt KK and twelve ways of being dealt AK. Thus, the chance that Peter had specifically KK was $3/(6 + 3 + 12) = 3/21 = 1/7 = 14.3\%$. So Joan's raise also made mathematical sense.

When Michelle check-raised Joan on the river, Joan wondered what Michelle might hold. Joan was convinced she was ahead of Peter; however, she felt it entirely possible that Michelle, a very loose player, would have called down the hand with TT. Joan was quite surprised when Michelle turned over 72o. While Joan could have re-raised Michelle, it's quite likely that had she done so Peter would have folded. All-in-all, Joan maximized her profit on this hand.

During a poker session we see a very limited number of premium hands. The chance of being dealt any specific pocket pair is just 221 to 1 (0.45%). On any specific hand, your chance of being dealt AA, KK, QQ, JJ, TT, AK, or AQ is 24.6 to 1 (4.1%). Add to this is the fact that some of the time you will lose with your premium hands.

Let's assume that you're dealt A♠A♥ and face one opponent who holds a random hand, and that the hand makes it to the river. The aces will win 85.4% of the time. Now assume you face eight opponents, all of whom stay through the river. The aces are still the most likely winner, but they only win 34.9% of the time. The table below summarizes how premium hands fare against one to eight opponents staying through the river.

You need to make the most of your good hands. After flopping a set, Joan maximized her win while Peter did not. When their premium hands were beaten, Joan lost as little as possible while Peter maximized his loss. Yes, they were both unlucky with their premium

Cards	1 Opp.	2 Opp.	3 Opp.	4 Opp.
A♠A♥	85.4%	73.6%	63.7%	55.9%
K♠K♥	82.3%	68.9%	58.3%	49.7%
Q♠Q♥	80.1%	65.3%	53.2%	44.8%
J♠J♥	77.2%	61.1%	49.1%	40.2%
T♠T♥	74.9%	57.5%	45.5%	36.3%
A♠K♠	67.2%	50.9%	41.4%	35.5%
A♠K♥	65.3%	48.2%	38.6%	32.6%
A♠Q♠	66.1%	49.3%	39.7%	33.8%
A♠Q♥	64.3%	47.1%	36.6%	30.1%

Cards	5 Opp.	6 Opp.	7 Opp.	8 Opp.
A♠A♥	49.1%	43.5%	38.4%	34.9%
K♠K♥	42.9%	37.4%	32.9%	29.3%
Q♠Q♥	38.0%	32.5%	28.4%	25.3%
J♠J♥	33.8%	28.5%	24.6%	21.6%
T♠T♥	29.5%	25.1%	21.7%	19.1%
A♠K♠	31.0%	27.7%	25.0%	22.5%
A♠K♥	28.1%	24.5%	21.6%	19.4%
A♠Q♠	29.2%	25.9%	23.3%	21.3%
A♠Q♥	26.2%	22.6%	19.8%	17.5%

hands, but is Joan a lucky player or a skillful player to maximize her win?

You cannot fear that the absolute nuts are out against you on every hand. There are occasions where you will flop middle set and be up against top set. You will lose a lot of money. Conversely, sometimes you will flop top set and be up against middle set, netting you a large pot. Over time, all the cards even out.

But that's *not* how Jerrod thought about Justin. Jerrod could not remember a single hand where he had beaten Justin at a showdown. He recalled, with amazing clarity, the back-to-back hands where Justin made a straight flush to beat his own ace-high flush and then flopped quads to beat his flopped boat. Additionally, Justin's egotistically superior attitude towards the world (and Jerrod) infuriated him. Jerrod tried to avoid sitting at Justin's table; however, in the following example, Justin was moved to Jerrod's table from the "must-move" game. Jerrod had no choice but to play with Justin or leave the game. He decided to play, and eventually an interesting hand occurred.

Four players, including Justin, had limped in their $8-$16 limit hold'em game. After the small blind folded, Jerrod looked down to see Q♠3♣ and checked his option. The pot had $80 after the rake. The flop came K♦T♥3♦, giving Jerrod bottom pair. With five players in the hand, Jerrod didn't think his hand was good. Additionally, he felt that bluffing at this pot with two cards in the playing zone was a horrible play. He checked, and was quite surprised when everyone behind him checked as well.

The turn was the Q♥. Jerrod had mixed feelings about this card. While it made him two pair, it was yet another card in the playing zone on the board. Now anyone with AJ would have a straight. Additionally, it put a second two-flush on the board. Still, Jerrod felt that he had to take a stab at the pot. If he were raised, he could reevaluate his hand. After all, his two pair could be the best hand.

So Jerrod fired a $16 bet into the pot, and after two players folded, Justin called. The remaining player folded, so it was heads-up going to the river in the battle for this $112 pot.

The river was the 3♠, giving Jerrod a full house. Even with Justin at the table, he was certain that he had the best hand, and he made the $16 bet. Justin quickly raised to $32. Jerrod just as quickly reraised to $48. Justin said, "I should re-raise you, but I feel nice today, so I'll just call." As he was calling, Justin casually flipped over his K♥3♥, and his full house beat Jerrod's full house.

Jerrod then went livid. He started trash-talking Justin, complaining about his bad play and how he won that hand because of luck, not skill. Justin sat silently and took the verbal assault, and during the next hour, Jerrod went on tilt and dropped $200 more on hands he should have folded but played just to get back at Justin.

Jerrod was angry about Justin's play in the example hand, but was he correct to call it poor? Justin flopped a great hand, but he knew he was vulnerable to a diamond. Sure, Justin should not have played the hand (K3s is not a hand you want to play); however, once he called pre-flop and then flopped a big hand (top and bottom pair), there was no way he was going to fold. Justin, by checking the flop, took the chance that someone would catch up to him.

Instead of bemoaning his fate (Jerrod indeed got unlucky on the hand in that he ran into K3), he should have been thrilled that Justin sat down at the table and voluntarily played a hand like K3s. If Justin continued with his poor starting hand selection, and Jerrod exercised *reasonable* judgment with his starting hands, then Jerrod figured to do quite well in this game. The poker proverb that money flows from the impatient to the patient is quite true. Instead, Jerrod went on tilt, played a bunch of hands just to get back at Justin, and became even more impatient than his least favorite opponent.

After Jerrod left the game, Michelle took his seat. That didn't bother Justin, but the other person who sat down really did—the new dealer, Tom. Justin couldn't remember the last time that he won a hand when Tom dealt to him. It wasn't that Tom was unfriendly, or acted like a jerk to him; rather, he got such horrendous cards and beats when Tom was the dealer. Justin ignored the fact that this cardroom, like most in the United States, had installed shuffling machines and all the dealer did (for the most part) was cut the cards and deal the hands.[40] Justin briefly considered getting up from the table and sitting out for the next thirty minutes until Tom was replaced with a new dealer, but he was up over $300 and everything was working. He was confident that even Tom couldn't ruin his day.

Justin was under the gun on Tom's first hand, and was shocked to see K♣K♦. He couldn't believe that Tom had actually dealt him a good hand. Justin raised to $16, and only Michelle (in the cutoff seat) and Joan (in the big blind) called. The pot was $48 (after the $4 in rake) going to the flop.

The flop came A♥T♦5♣. Joan immediately bet $8 and Justin was faced with a decision. *It figured that Tom put out the ace,* Justin thought. After thinking for a few more seconds, he concluded that Joan had an ace and he folded. Joan not only had an ace, but also a ten (she held A♠T♠) and won the hand, beating Michelle's 7♣7♥. After the hand was completed, Justin launched a tirade at the dealer. "Can't you ever put out a flop without an ace when I have pocket kings?" Justin asked. "It's like you're out to get me."

Sure, Justin was unlucky that an ace came on the flop. However, he should have looked at the positive aspects of the hand. First, the ace

---

[40]Casinos and cardrooms installed shuffling machines because they increase the number of hands dealt per hour, thus increasing the casino's rake.

came on the flop, not the river when he would have had more money invested in the hand. Second, had he not been so angry at the dealer he would have noticed that Michelle stayed in the hand to the showdown with just a pair of sevens, even after there had been a pre-flop raiser and two overcards on the flop.

But blaming the dealer is ridiculous. Most dealers handle their jobs professionally, dealing the cards, keeping control over their table, and keeping the games moving. They have no control over the cards you get. Indeed, professional dealers get upset when they make mistakes. After all, their livelihood depends on the tips that they receive from the players (dealers are paid a low hourly wage and receive most of their compensation through tips).

Too many people today blame others before they turn inwards and review their own actions. If you play poker, you *will* both give and get bad beats. It's inevitable. It's part of the game. However, luck evens out in the long run. There are sessions that you play that will end up on the credit side of the ledger no matter what. Even then, ask yourself if you limited your loss to the minimum possible. Conversely, there are days that you *will* be a winner. But did you maximize your win? The lucky players out there did just that.

Losing Because You Don't Use Game Selection

Aaron walked into his local cardroom, wondering what game he should play. A reasonably skilled limit hold'em player, he saw that all of the low and mid-limit hold'em games had long lists. When he asked the *brush* (the person who runs the interest boards in a cardroom) whether any new games would start soon, she told him, "Not for another hour, at least. Many of our dealers are in a mandatory training meeting." He put his name on the $6-$12 and $8-$16 lists, and also on the $100 no-limit list solely because that list was very short. He would prefer almost anything to no-limit hold'em, but it appeared it was only his choice at this casino today. Five minutes later, he found himself in a $1/$2 blind $100 fixed buy-in no-limit game.

The empty seat was right behind the button, so he immediately posted and got a hand.[41] Everyone folded to Nolan, who raised to $10 from middle position. Joan, sitting next to Nolan, called. There were two more folds, and Mrs. Goldman, sitting to the right of Aaron, also called. Aaron peeked at his cards and saw Q♣9♣, considered the pot odds, and called. The small blind folded, but Mick in the big blind raised to $50. Aaron noticed that Mick had over $300 in his stack. All of the other players folded, and after re-evaluating his hand, Aaron made the wise decision to fold.

Aaron folded his next four hands (he was dealt trash hands). On two of them, Mick made substantial raises. On one of them, Joan made

---

[41]Some casinos require new players to post a bet, equal to the size of the big blind, to receive their first hand. This rule is *not* universal, so you should always ask how your cardroom handles this situation.

a big raise holding pocket eights. On the final hand, Mrs. Goldman called down Nolan's AKo with pocket deuces and won a $120 pot. Aaron continued to get trash hands and folded each and every hand until his big blind.

There's nothing particularly unusual about this sequence. Indeed, plays like these are made hundreds of times each day in cardrooms and on the Internet. Perhaps you're wondering why we picked this particular example. Well, it highlights how Aaron needlessly lost $8 in a game he really didn't want to play.

When Aaron got to that table, he played his first hand without any knowledge of his opponents. Being a limit hold'em specialist, he had rarely played against these opponents. In fact, had he observed the table as he did on the next four hands, he would have discovered that Mick was a maniac making many very large raises, that Mrs. Goldman was a calling station, and that Joan liked making big raises with medium pocket pairs. Wouldn't that have been good information to have *before* he sat down?

All he had to do to obtain that information was *not* play that hand. Aaron could have—should have—made an excuse (using the restroom, making a phone call, etc.), and then observed the action for a few minutes before playing any hands. Had he done so, he would have saved $8. As a solid player, Aaron would have known *not* to play his Q♣9♣ when a re-raise was likely.

Of course, we do need to ask ourselves another question: why did Aaron sit down in a game he didn't want to play? No one put a gun to his head and made him play in that game. Indeed, one hour later when the meeting was over, Aaron got into an $8-$16 limit hold'em game. Although his foray into no-limit cost him *only* $40, had he waited for the $8-$16 game or driven three miles to the other local cardroom and played there, he'd still have that $40.

In this chapter, we'll explore the decisions you make when you enter a game. We will look at the game you choose, the table you choose, and your opponents. We'll also discuss when you should leave the game, and the reasons why you should (and shouldn't) depart.

Game selection is highly dependent upon the cardroom you play in. Some cardrooms have four or five tables, and the choice is between playing $3-$6 limit hold'em or not playing at all. If you live in the Los Angeles area, the major cardrooms all have a huge number of games at almost any limit you can think of (and plenty of no-limit action, too). Many of the Las Vegas casinos now feature large poker rooms, giving the player a wide choice of games. Of course, if you play on the Internet, the major sites all feature a large number of hold'em tables at many limits.

But if your main game is *not* hold'em, you'll face a limited choice. Seven-card stud used to be king on the east coast; however, hold'em is the undisputed leader now across the country. There may be only one or two stud games (or Omaha, if that's your game of choice) to choose from. That's not much of a selection.

If you do play stud or Omaha, you will probably face many of the same players day after day. That's not necessarily a bad thing—most Omaha players, for example, play quite poorly. An obvious point is that if you are (or become) a winning player in stud or Omaha, you need to treat your opponents with courtesy and decorum. *These are the people who are paying your wages,* after all; scaring them away from the table is the last thing you want to do.

Once you decide what game you're going to play, you must decide on a limit (or, for no-limit hold'em, a blind structure). Do you remember what happened to Chris in Chapter 10, *Losing Because You Don't Have an Adequate Bankroll*, beginning on page 83 when he played in the "big game?" We strongly recommend that you play at a level you are comfortable with.

But what should you do if the lists are incredibly long? There isn't much you can do other than to wait it out or head home. If you play in a game you're uncomfortable playing in, you will likely lose. There's a solution to this, though—learn another game.

We especially like Omaha high/low as a good game to learn for several reasons. First, correct play in Omaha is tight, so you'll be able to observe a lot of hands. Second, at the low limits play is usually quite loose, making these games beatable. And third, you will usually find low limit Omaha high/low being spread in many cardrooms.

No matter what game becomes your second choice, start at a low limit so you can learn the game. Consider your first few sessions as part of your tuition as you start your new venture. Playing at very low limits will lessen the cost of the mistakes that you will undoubtedly make. Consider playing on the Internet, where many sites have limits as low as 2¢-4¢.

But what should you do if you get to the cardroom and all the lists are ridiculously long except for a game you hate? We've faced that situation, and we voted with our feet: we left. We're not going to play out of our comfort zone. It leads to losing sessions. Luckily, when this happened to us, we were able to either walk or make a short drive to a different cardroom with a better selection.

Now let's return to Aaron, who finally got into the game he wanted: $8-$16 limit hold'em. Even better for Aaron, his eight opponents were all poor players. Aaron quickly won $80, turning his $40 loss for the day into a $40 profit. But then one of his opponents looked at his watch, made some remark about meeting his wife, and left the game. And then another departed. Soon all eight of his opponents were replaced by new opponents.

Aaron recognized all of his new opponents as players who normally play $20-$40 hold'em or higher. And they were playing deadly serious poker. He had no idea what they were doing in his (relatively) low-limit game, but he wasn't happy. Aaron took a break from his game and asked the floorman to put him on the *change list* for a different table (in some cardrooms, this is called the *table change* list). Within fifteen minutes, Aaron found himself in a game with what he would term "the usual suspects."

What Aaron did was intelligent. He found himself in a game where he was facing all experts (relative to his ability). He could have continued in this game; if he were *very* lucky, he'd find himself a winner for the day. Or he could change tables (or games) and almost assuredly face weaker opposition and have a much better chance of winning.

If you play online poker, this is much easier. There are so many games offered at the low and middle limits that when you find yourself in a bad game, it's almost always easy to leave your seat and enter a different game at the same limits (or blinds). Indeed, not only is it simple to exit such a game, it's much easier to track and play against your weaker opponents.

If you play online, use the note-taking feature that your site has so you'll know the characteristics of your opponents. When we find particularly poor opponents, we add them to our buddy lists. At a later date when we log on to the site, we can check if one of these players is currently in a game. This way, we can spot the easy games much faster.

A tremendous tool for recognizing these poor players is *Poker-Tracker*. If you play online, it's a must-buy. It keeps track of numerous statistics, and allows you (through the use of your computer) to find some of these generous opponents.

If you play on the Internet, you should also evaluate your own play using *PokerTracker*. The data you can obtain from PokerTracker on your own play is invaluable. There are literally hundreds of different statistics on your own play (as well as the play of any opponent you've ever faced). This information will tell you more about your game than any casual observer ever could, and it will allow you to make countless strategy adjustments and improvements to your game.

In order to improve your game you should also track your results by game and level. You may find that you're a winner in $4-$8 and $8-$16 hold'em but not in $6-$12 hold'em. You then have to determine why your results vary. Are you playing differently in $6-$12? Are you facing better opponents? Or is it just the vagaries of chance?

If you play online and use *PokerTracker*, you can scan your results and see if there's a difference in how you're playing your hands. If you combine *PokerTracker* with a results tracking program such as *StatKing*, you will always know exactly where you stand.

Something to remember is that it takes a large number of hands to develop an accurate sample size to measure your results. This should be obvious—you'll have a much better idea after playing 1,000 hands than 100 hands, and after playing 100,000 hands than 1,000 hands. As mentioned in Chapter 14, *Losing Because You're Playing in Tournaments*, beginning on page 122, this is a consequence of the Central Limit Theorem.[42]

As you play more hands, your results will become more indicative of your playing ability. Let's assume that you've just begun to play

$8-$16 hold'em. In your first session, you have a great day, everything goes your way, and you win $1,200 in three hours. Is it likely you'll keep up a $400/hour win-rate? Of course not—that's unsustainable for even the best players. Only after you play thousands of hands will you know what your true win rate is. One particularly lucky session should never be used to judge your ability in a game. Unfortunately, you will also have unlucky days where you'll be the victim of every possible bad beat.

Bad beats happen to everyone. It's what we do *after* suffering a bad beat that separates good players from bad. Consider this hand played by Jerrod. He had just suffered a horrendous beat when Mrs. Goldman (who can put anyone on tilt) hit her two-outer and took down a huge $470 pot in an $8-$16 game. She was still stacking her chips (and would likely be doing so for some time), when the dealer told her that she was under-the-gun and must act first. She limped, as did Joan and Mick from middle position. Jerrod, on the button, looked down at 4♠4♣. He raised, the blinds folded, and the limpers all called. There was $72 in the pot heading to the flop (four players at $16 each, plus $12 from the blinds, less $4 raked from the pot).

The flop came T♠8♠2♠. Mrs. Goldman checked, Joan bet, and Mick folded. Jerrod raised, figuring he could use his position to bully the pot into his win column. Mrs. Goldman looked at the board, and back at her hand, and the board, and again at her hand, trying to decide what to do. After a few moments, she called; Joan quickly called. There was $120 in the pot.

The turn was the 7♦. Mrs. Goldman and Joan checked, and Jerrod bet. Mrs. Goldman took time out from stacking her chips (from the last hand) to *attempt* to concentrate on what she should do. After lots of fidgeting, she called. Joan also called. The pot had grown to $168.

The river was the 4♥, giving Jerrod a set of fours. Mrs. Goldman looked at the 4, and then at her hand, and at the 4, and back to her hand, and finally *bet* the river. Joan mucked her hand, and it was clear from Joan's facial expression that her flush draw had not come in. Jerrod considered whether or not he should raise. After all, he

---

[42] See footnote 37 on page 127. For sample sizes, the larger the sample size (as *n* approaches infinity), the better the sample results represent the actual population.

was up against Mrs. Goldman. He decided that his set was likely better than whatever she held, and he did raise to $32. Mrs. Goldman looked back down at her cards, and said to Jerrod, "Oh, so you do have the flush. Well, I'll pay you off." She threw the extra $16 into the pot, and flipped over her 6♥5♠, giving her an 8-high straight. Jerrod angrily slid his cards into the muck, as Mrs. Goldman began adding the $232 pot into her steadily growing stack (now consisting mostly of Jerrod's chips).

Jerrod made plenty of mistakes on this hand. His pre-flop raise wasn't that bad a play. Indeed, he succeeded in driving out the blinds. However, he was facing three relatively loose opponents, and he would likely have to hit something in order to win the pot.

The flop was a disaster for Jerrod. His 4-high flush draw was worthless. Additionally, the flop featured two cards in the playing zone. Instead of raising on the flop, he should have folded. The turn added yet another overcard, but Jerrod continued to bet.

When Mrs. Goldman bet on the river, it was clear from her actions that she hit *something*. While this could have been two pair (say, T4s), it wasn't likely. After all, only one 4 remained in the deck. It was much more likely that she hit a draw. The only draw she could have hit on the river was 65, giving her a straight. Jerrod should have been able to cut his losses.

However, the key to the hand wasn't Jerrod's play on the flop, turn, or river. Rather, it was his psychological condition when he started the hand. His head wasn't in the game; he was on tilt from the previous hand. While many of us can take a bad beat in stride and correctly play the next hand, Jerrod couldn't. He should have taken a break from the game for a few minutes. Had he done so, he wouldn't have made any errors on the hand because he wouldn't have played it in the first place.

Being on tilt, like the game getting bad, is a good reason to get up from a game. Another reason to leave a game is when you're tired. As we mentioned on page 100, playing while tired is like playing while drunk. We've seen many players build a big stack, become tired, and give it all back. *The games will be there tomorrow.*

Should you lock up a big win? Suppose you're up a large amount, but the game is still very good and you're likely to increase your win. You've been playing for hours, but the donators are still donating. One strategy is to mentally place a portion of your win, say $400 out of $500, as "locked up." Continue playing your normal game, but if your stack begins to decline, when it approaches a $400 win, rack up and leave the game. In theory, it's best to continue playing while you have an advantage. However, there's a *psychological* benefit to having big wins—you gain confidence in your game. In fact, if you've been struggling and have had many losing sessions in a row, locking up even a small win helps your poker psychological well-being.

A special situation that should be mentioned is *must-move* games. Sometimes these games are quite good in their own right; however, there are occasions where the must-move game is tight while the main game is excellent. We'll stay in a bad must-move game if we will either make a good main game soon or if it is likely that the must-move game will improve based on the players who are on the board for the game.

Today, we're blessed in the poker world to be playing in generally great games at all levels. Many of our opponents play as if their results are irrelevant; some play as if they're handing you blank checks. When you get in a bad game, or you're not playing well in a good game, getting up from the game will save you money and help your psyche.

Losing Because You've Forgotten the Goal of Poker

Why do you play poker? Why does anyone play poker? We learned poker in college as a mainly social activity. We made friends with people who lived in the dorms, and perhaps made a dollar or two (it was hard to make much money at the penny-ante stakes we played). Sometimes we still play poker for the social aspect. We both play in home games that have expanded our business networks, where the stakes are so small that they're irrelevant for us today.

Some people play poker to supplement their income. That's why Aaron plays. He's good enough to win in his usual game, and he's usually smart enough to avoid games he'd lose in. He enjoys playing, and he's used some of his winnings on a new home entertainment system.

Some play because it's the "in" thing to do. That's the case for many of the college-aged students, like Justin, who have taken up the game in huge numbers. They see their poker heroes easily winning on television, and they want to emulate them. So they either head off to the casino or play online, just *knowing* that they will win too. A lot of parents of students will be surprised to find out where their kids' allowances have gone. Because they think they already know everything, many of these players don't care about learning anything new.

A few play because their spouses have dragged them off to the casino. They're bored, and they need something to do. That's the case for Mrs. Goldman. Her husband had the sense to hire her a tutor, so that she'd have a chance at the tables. If only she could learn....

You will find people playing poker because it's a way to release their competitive energies. This is true for Joan. She was a varsity athlete while at college, and now instead of fighting it out on the basketball court, she's battling on the felt. This type of player tends to be quite aggressive. When these players are able to reign in some of their aggression, they can become very strong poker players.

There are some players who are just passing the time. These are usually *nits,* players who are super-tight. They're playing for the comps and the free drinks, and are generally social players. They're typically on a budget, and staying within that budget is paramount. Their goal is to win a dollar or lose a dollar.

There are also players who play by rote. They've learned *one* way of playing, and for them, that's the *only* way to tackle a hand. Typically, they learn a set of starting hands from a book, and that's how they'll play that hand in every situation. These players tend to win when they're up against weak opposition but they have severe difficulties when they face skilled opponents.

Some play just for the entertainment. While they'd rather win, they place a higher importance on having fun. Many of these players end up being maniacs, raising at any opportunity (like Mick) because they have the need to be noticed. These players are found in high-limit games, too.

Of course, there are professional poker players. Some of these players are grinders, playing in the low middle-limit games ($10-$20 to $20-$40), content on playing thirty to forty hours each week, and earning a specific sum each year. You'll find them online, and in areas where there is a major concentration of casinos and card-rooms—Atlantic City, Las Vegas, and Southern California, for example.

There are also tournament specialists, who have large bankrolls (or arc backed) and usually tremendous acumen for these events. They travel from city to city playing in the major tournaments. Only a few tournament specialists, such as Doyle Brunson, also do well in ring games; different skills and abilities are needed for each.

Each of these kinds of players will handle a poker hand differently. Let's look at a sample hand, and note the differences. It's a nine-handed $8-$16 limit hold'em game, two players have folded, and you're in middle position holding J♣T♠. This is your first hand in a casino where you know no one, so you have no reads on your opponents. What would you do?

Aaron would fold this hand from middle position. He doesn't know anything about his opponents and there are too many people left to act. It's far too dangerous to commit any chips to this hand.

Justin, our "look" player, would raise. He's watched all the pros on the *World Poker Tour* and the *World Series of Poker* raise with this hand, and if they can do it, so can he.

There's no reason to try to figure out what Mrs. Goldman would do. If her poker coach had just told her about JT, she might raise; but then again, she might just call if her husband was watching her play. Or she might fold because she was involved in a discussion with the person sitting next to her. Reasoning out why she does anything at the poker table is nearly impossible.

Joan would raise with the JT. It's a playable hand, she's first in the pot, and it's possible her raise could buy the hand. The fact that she's going to be out of position for the rest of the hand doesn't enter her mind.

The nits of the world would fold without thinking. From middle position, AA is playable, KK is marginal, and QQ is very borderline. Indeed, they would likely fold JTo from any position except an unraised big blind.

The rote players would compare the hand to the hand chart they've memorized. If they're using the hand chart from *Hold'em Poker for Advanced Players*,[43] they will call with this hand. Given the lack of knowledge of their opponents, this is *not* a bad play. Unfortunately, these players will still play JTo the same way three hours later when they do have a lot of information on their opponents.

Mick would raise because it meets his standards: two cards above a six (his raises with 52o have been particularly disastrous). It's the first hand, and he might as well let everyone know that he's going to have fun today.

---

[43]Sklansky, David, and Mason Malmuth, *Hold'em Poker for Advanced Players: 21st Century Edition*, Henderson, NV: Two Plus Two Publishing, 1999. The hand chart is on pages 15 and 16. The discussion of what hands to play from middle position is on pages 27-31.

A professional would likely fold this hand in this situation. Like Nolan, he'd judge that it's a bit too dangerous to act with JTo in *early* middle position against unknown opponents.

We're not critiquing any of these plays. We mention all of them because, when you're sitting at a poker table, *you* should be analyzing how your opponents play and understanding *why* they act in the way that they do. Once you grasp an individual's motivation, you're well on the way to besting that person in the game.

If you want to win more (or lose less) while playing poker, your motivation *must* become money-driven. You must look at each session as a way of increasing your bankroll at the expense of your opposition. Sure, there will be occasions when you're playing for fun in a home game or with friends and you don't care about your results, but when you walk into a cardroom, the most important question you should ask is, "How can I make the most money today?"

Every action you make should have that as its underlying goal. Most importantly, treat your opponents as you would want to be treated. Remember, you're in the customer service industry. Make everyone feel comfortable and welcome at your table. Make it your goal to put a smile on each face. And whatever outlandish plays you see made, never, *ever* chastise another player. Scaring away paying customers is just bad business.

Watch top cash game pros at the table. They're considerate of their opposition, talking to them about various subjects, sympathizing with them when they make their inevitable blunders, and congratulating them when they hit their two-outers. Yes, we're aware that some tournament pros berate their opponents, saying things like, "How can you make that play? Staying in the hand for runner-runner...." *Don't fall into that trap!*

How do you make money playing poker? You can get lucky and have the deck run over you. This happens to everyone, and when it does, you'll be a big winner. You can play against opponents who make many mistakes relative to you; usually you'll end up winning. Or you can play a more skillful game than your opposition. Here, too, you should end up a winner.

Most poker players are losers. As we wrote in *Mastering No-Limit Hold'em*, the rake ensures that *at least* 85% of players are losers.[44] You must treat your fellow players as a valuable asset, because they are. Without them, you'd have to rely on luck in order to win. Over time, we all hold the same cards; living off of luck is futile in the long run.

You may be thinking that we're crazy; you're not in the customer service business, the casino is. While the casino must make sure that you are happy playing in the cardroom, it's your responsibility to make your fellow players happy. If you follow the Golden Rule—don't criticize, condemn, or complain—you're most of the way there. Emulate the cash game pros, and you'll be surprised how much longer your losing opponents stay in your game.[45]

We've come full circle, and are back at the question we posed to start this chapter: Why do you play poker? If you're venturing into a cardroom, or playing on the Internet, there's only one valid answer: to make money. Sure, you should have fun while you're playing, but until your goal is increasing your income, you'll likely find yourself a loser.

---

[44]Fox, Russell and Scott T. Harker, *Mastering No-Limit Hold'em*, Pittsburgh, PA: Conjelco, 2005, pp. 122-125.

[45]We feel so strongly about this that we re-read customer service books. One of our favorites, *The Real Heroes of Business—and Not a CEO Among Them*, is listed in our bibliography.

Twenty Hands at the Cardroom

Introduction

This game never happened. But the hands described all took place.

When we started writing this book, we considered showing twenty actual hands (two orbits at a ten-handed table). As we looked over records of hands we've played and have seen, we could not find twenty consecutive hands (or, for that matter, ten consecutive hands) that would hold your interest. Instead, we've adopted real hands that are interesting.

We're using the ten characters we've previously described to bet and play these hands. These are the kinds of players you will find today in cardrooms and playing on the Internet. We have modified the betting and actions to match the characters, but the hands are real.

While you may believe that these characters cannot be *collectively* found where you play poker, we face players like this whenever we play. Indeed, every one of these characters is drawn from our experiences at the table.

The floorman calls our players to a brand new $5-$10 limit hold'em game.[46] Most of our players buy in for $300; however, Peter buys in for only $100 and Nolan and Aaron buy in for $500.

The Players

Seat 1 – Mrs. Goldman. Mrs. Goldman tries to play well. Her husband has paid for lessons with a world-class tutor. Unfortunately,

---

[46]This particular cardroom has a bet and three raise rule and rakes each hand 10% to $4 maximum.

the saying "a little knowledge is a dangerous thing" can be applied to her actions at the card table. She accurately remembers bits and pieces of what her tutor has told her. Today, her husband and her tutor are seated behind the rail watching her actions.

Seat 2 – Peter. Peter is a relatively new player, and tends to play a weak/tight brand of poker. When he's in over his head he'll play like a nit.

Seat 3 – Chris. Chris is a new player, and he considers himself to be the unluckiest player in the world.

Seat 4 – Jerrod. Jerrod plays tight poker, so tight that his friends have accused him of squeaking when he throws chips into the pot. He's recently taken up no-limit hold'em, because he likes the fact that he can make big money when he gets big pairs.

Seat 5 – Michelle. While Jerrod plays tight, Michelle plays loose. She loves to see flops, because any two cards can win. If the pot's unraised, it's a rare hand that she'll fold.

Seat 6 – Nolan. Nolan plays like a professional. He can play almost any style of game, and is generally a tight/aggressive player. He's only in today's game to help his friend Chris; they're planning a critique session following the game. Normally you would find Nolan in a much higher game.

Seat 7 – Joan. Joan loves no-limit hold'em, where she can say her two favorite words, "All in." She's loose and aggressive, but not a complete maniac at the table as she's *slightly* cautious post-flop.

Seat 8 – Mick. While Joan tends towards playing like a maniac, Mick *is* a maniac. Almost any two cards will do. He loves to raise with nothing.

Seat 9 – Aaron. Aaron is a solid limit hold'em player. He's tight and aggressive and ready to move up to his cardroom's $15-$30 game. However, he is just learning how to play no-limit hold'em.

Seat 10 – Justin. Justin learned the game on the Internet, and has only recently started to play live poker. He finds the game slow in the cardroom, and can get bored waiting for hands to play out. When he's bored, he'll liven up the game. He always wears sunglasses, a baseball cap, and a sweatshirt from his college.

The following hands begin the action in a tabular format. Follow the action going from top to bottom in the Pre-Flop Action column. If there is continued action around the table (raises, calls of raises, re-raises, etc.) they will be listed in subsequent columns. Also note that the player who is the button is indicated by parenthesis and italics.

After the flop, the action will described and an in-depth analysis will be presented. Finally, after each hand, we will keep track of the chip stacks of all the players so you can see who is winning and losing throughout the session.

The dealer spreads the cards, and the players draw for the placement of the button on the first hand. Mrs. Goldman picks the A♠, so the button is in seat one for the first hand.

Hands 1 – 10 (Ten Limit Hold'em Hands)

Hand 1.	Blinds $2/$5			
Players	Cards	Pre-Flop Action		
Jerrod	8♥7♦	fold		
Michelle	J♥7♥	call $5	call $15 total	
Nolan	9♦4♠	fold		
Joan	K♣J♠	raise to $10	call $15 total	
Mick	T♣7♣	re-raise to $15		
Aaron	Q♣8♣	fold		
Justin	Q♠J♣	call $15		
(Mrs. Goldman)	6♣5♣	call $15		
Peter ($2 sb)	T♥3♦	fold		
Chris ($5 bb)	K♦9♥	fold		

Michelle spots the J♥7♥ and sees that they're suited and limps. Joan raises with K♣J♠, a great hand from her perspective. Mick has the T♣7♣ and re-raises. After all, they're suited. Justin calls with his Q♠J♣. Mrs. Goldman looks down at the 6♣5♦, sees that they're connected and makes the easy call. Michelle and Joan quickly call the raises. There's $78 in the pot going to the flop ($4 is taken for the rake).

The flop comes 2♣T♠6♥. Michelle checks. Joan bets (two over-cards is a solid hand!). Mick makes the no-brainer raise to $10 with his top pair. Justin, annoyed with the flop, folds. Mrs. Goldman goes into a trance, finally deciding that a pair is good and makes the call. Michelle sees that all she has is a backdoor flush draw and folds. Joan calls the raise. There's $108 in the pot.

The turn is the 4♣, giving Mick a flush draw and Mrs. Goldman a one-card straight draw. Joan, realizing that all she holds are over-cards, checks. Mick quickly bets $10. Mrs. Goldman calls and Joan starts thinking. After a few moments, she folds. The pot is now $128.

The river is the 3♠, giving Mrs. Goldman the straight. But Mick still thinks he's ahead and bets $10. Mrs. Goldman looks at the 3, back at her hand, at the 3 again, and raises to $20. Mick can't believe that the 3 helped her, but having played against Mrs. Goldman in the past, he realizes that she could hold anything and just calls.

Mrs. Goldman turns over her 6-high straight and takes down the $168 pot.

Analysis. Calling from early position with two *random* suited cards is a good way to lose money, as Michelle finds out on this hand. She's out of position, so she almost has to flop perfect cards in order to win the pot. Had she folded pre-flop, she would have saved $15. *That $15 equates to half the hourly win rate for a good player in this game!* Mick, our resident maniac, wouldn't listen to anyone about how he plays his hands. He fell into the same trap as Michelle on this hand and finds his stack $105 lower because he played a trash hand—*but they were suited!*

Mrs. Goldman's actions aren't as bad as you might think. She has position on this hand, which is vital. Her 65o figures to be live. When the flop comes ten-high rainbow, her middle pair *is* a good holding if she's not up against a pocket pair. Small connected cards *in position* can be great cards when you can see a flop cheaply. Yes, Mrs. Goldman should have folded her hand, but once she saw the flop her actions weren't that bad (of course, she had no idea of that).

Chip Stacks: Mrs. Goldman $413; Peter: $98; Chris: $295; Jerrod: $300; Michelle: $285; Nolan: $500; Joan: $275; Mick: $245; Aaron: $500; Justin: $285

Hand 2.	Blinds $2/$5			
Players	Cards	Pre-Flop Action		
Michelle	K♠4♠	fold		
Nolan	A♥Q♣	raise to $10	re-raise to $20	
Joan	2♥2♠	calls	call $20 total	
Mick	A♣7♠	re-raise to $15	call $20 total	
Aaron	T♦8♦	fold		
Justin	A♦7♣	fold		
Mrs. Goldman	Q♥J♥	call $15	call $20 total	
(Peter)	A♠4♣	fold		
Chris ($2 sb)	8♥2♣	fold		
Jerrod ($5 bb)	Q♠7♥	fold		

Nolan has A♥Q♣, and raises to $10. Joan looks down at 2♥2♠, a real hand, and calls. Mick has A♣7♠, and with the ace makes the obvious re-raise. Aaron folds, and Justin reluctantly folds his A♦7♣. Mrs. Goldman has Q♥J♥, and knows that it's a strong hand, and calls. Everyone else folds. The betting returns to Nolan. Nolan elects to cap the betting with his AQo. Those remaining in the hand call. There's $83 in the pot.

The flop comes 6♥T♣3♥, giving Mrs. Goldman a flush draw, although Joan is still in the lead with her underpair. Nolan believes that it's likely the flop hasn't helped anyone and bets $5. Joan hesitates and calls. Mick also believes that the flop hasn't helped anyone and raises to $10. Mrs. Goldman spots her flush draw and calls the two bets. Nolan elects to just call, as does Joan. The pot has grown to $123.

The turn is the 5♣, helping no one. Nolan elects to make one more attempt to win the pot, and bets $10. Joan, still with the lone pair of deuces and looking at four overcards, believes that Nolan has a pocket pair and folds. Mick simply calls with just an ace. Mrs. Goldman elects to call with her flush draw. The pot now stands at $153.

The river is the 9♦ and Nolan is first to act. With everyone calling, he believes that someone has *something* and decides to check. Mick believes that a bet might win him the hand and puts out $10. Mrs. Goldman sees that she got a straight draw on the river but decides to fold anyway. Nolan, knowing that Mick is a maniac, decides to call believing that there's about a 25% chance that his ace-queen is high. Mick turns over his A7, but Nolan's AQ takes down the $173 pot.

Analysis. When a solid player like Nolan raises *from early position*, you need a good hand to continue. Had Mick folded, he would have $50 more in his stack. Joan's call with pocket deuces in early position was also poor. Small pocket pairs are difficult to play—you usually have to flop a set to continue with them. She should have folded either pre-flop or on the flop.

Somehow, Mrs. Goldman played the hand decently. Given her position, calling with the high suited connectors was a reasonable play. While folding pre-flop would also be acceptable (given that the first raise came from a good player in early position), her post-flop actions were correct. With the flush draw and two overcards, calling to the river was a sensible decision.

Chip Stacks: Mrs. Goldman $373; Peter: $98; Chris: $293; Jerrod: $295; Michelle: $285; Nolan: $623; Joan: $245; Mick: $195; Aaron: $500; Justin: $285

Hand 3.	Blinds $2/$5		
Players	Cards	Pre-Flop Action	
Nolan	8♠5♦	folds	
Joan	8♦7♦	raise to $10	call $15 total
Mick	J♠J♥	re-raise to $15	
Aaron	9♦2♣	fold	
Justin	9♠4♠	fold	
Mrs. Goldman	3♠3♦	call $15	
Peter	K♦K♥	call $15	
(Chris)	6♦4♥	fold	
Jerrod ($2 sb)	A♦8♣	fold	
Michelle ($5 bb)	Q♥4♣	fold	

Nolan folds, but Joan, holding suited connectors (8♦7♦), makes the easy raise to $10. Mick wakes up with J♠J♥ and re-raises to $15. Aaron and Justin fold, but Mrs. Goldman, knowing that any pair is a big hand, calls with her 3♠3♦. Peter peeks at this cards and can't believe he has K♦K♥. He thinks that with all this raising someone may hold aces and just calls. Everyone else folds, and Joan decides to call the re-raise. There's $63 in the pot.

The flop comes 6♥J♦Q♠, giving Mick a set. Joan, with only a backdoor draw, checks. Mick bets his set. Mrs. Goldman, still knowing that any pair might win, calls. Peter, still fearing aces, just calls. Joan reluctantly folds. There's $78 in the pot.

The turn is the 2♠, helping no one. Mick bets $10 and Mrs. Goldman calls—after all, she can still make trips on the river, and Peter now decides to raise with his overpair. Mick, holding his set, makes it three bets. Mrs. Goldman sighs and folds. Knowing he's up against aces, Peter folds, and Mick takes down the $138 pot.

Analysis. Joan's raise with 8♦7♦ from early position was a losing action. Playing suited connectors from early position will cost you money; *raising* with them will cost you even more money. Mick's pre-flop re-raise with jacks is correct, but Peter should have capped the betting with his kings. You can't play scared poker and win. Peter should have realized that against a maniac his kings were likely the best hand. Mrs. Goldman reverts to form and calls three bets with a small pocket pair.

Peter should not have folded on the turn when Mick re-raised Peter's check raise. As the cards lie, Peter was behind. Indeed, the flop was very dangerous with two cards in the playing zone. Given the nature of the flop, we would have raised *on the flop* to drive out as many players as possible. While Peter's fold was correct given that he was facing a set (he had two outs on the river, and needed 14 to 1 odds to have the right price to draw), *it was much more likely that Peter was ahead on the hand since he was up against a maniac.* Results-wise, Peter did the right thing; poker-wise, Peter should have called the re-raise and check-called the river.

Chip Stacks: Mrs. Goldman $343; Peter: $58; Chris: $293; Jerrod: $293; Michelle: $280; Nolan: $623; Joan: $230; Mick: $283; Aaron: $500; Justin: $285

Hand 4.	Blinds $2/$5			
Players	**Cards**	Pre-Flop Action		
Joan	A♦8♣	call $5		
Mick	K♠6♦	fold		
Aaron	Q♦4♥	fold		
Justin	9♦2♣	fold		
Mrs. Goldman	7♥4♦	call $5		
Peter	Q♠9♠	fold		
Chris	Q♣4♠	fold		
(Jerrod)	T♣2♠	fold		
Michelle ($2 sb)	Q♥6♣	call $5 total		
Nolan ($5 bb)	8♥4♣	checks		

Joan decides to limp with her A♦8♣. Everyone folds to Mrs. Goldman, who, with 7♥4♦, knows that she can make a straight and calls. It's folded to Michelle decides to call with Q♥6♣ and Nolan checks his option with 8♥4♣. There's $18 in the pot.

The flop comes 5♦5♥K♥ improving no one's hand. Michelle and Nolan quickly check. Joan, sensing weakness, bets with her one overcard. Mrs. Goldman encouraged that she only needs two more cards to make a straight, calls. Michelle and Nolan fold. The pot has inched up to $28.

The turn is the 6♥, giving Mrs. Goldman both a straight and a flush draw. Joan continues her attempt to bully Mrs. Goldman out of the pot and bets $10. Mrs. Goldman, seeing the straight draw (but not noticing the flush draw), calls. The pot is up to $46 after the rake.

The river is the J♥, giving Mrs. Goldman the flush. Joan decides enough is enough and checks. Mrs. Goldman notices that she has missed her straight and checks. Joan turns over her cards and says "ace high" as she displays A♦8♣. Mrs. Goldman, sighs, and says, "I only have a 7," and turns over her 7♥4♦. The dealer pushes Mrs. Goldman the $46 pot, as her flush takes it down. Mrs. Goldman stacks her chips still trying to determine why she won the pot.

Analysis. There are three points that can be taken from this hand. First, in a poker session you will play many hands where the flop misses everyone. Whoever ends up "buying the button" (the person last to act in each round of betting) has a huge advantage. They can bet *representing* a made hand (or a hand that has hit the flop) and take down many pots. Second, it's hard to bully the pot when you're first to act. Joan tried to get Mrs. Goldman to fold. However, she had two draws on the turn. When you're up against a player who will act like a calling station when he or she has any sort of draw, it's the time to stop bullying. That's the third point of this hand. Had Mrs. Goldman realized that she had a flush—and had Joan been aware of this, then Joan should have checked. However, Mrs. Goldman did *not* realize that she had a flush. Had Joan bet the river, she would have taken down the pot. So you do need to know when you're up against a player who might fold the winning hand. Needless to say, it also pays to read your cards so you know where *you* stand. However, as we've said before, that's just not one of Mrs. Goldman's abilities.

Chip Stacks: Mrs. Goldman $369; Peter: $58; Chris: $293; Jerrod: $293; Michelle: $275; Nolan: $618; Joan: $210; Mick: $283; Aaron: $500; Justin: $285

Hand 5.	Blinds $2/$5			
Players	Cards	Pre-Flop Action		
Mick	J♠T♦	raise to $10	call $15 total	
Aaron	K♠J♣	fold		
Justin	A♣2♦	call $10	call $15 total	
Mrs. Goldman	T♥7♠	fold		
Peter	6♥3♠	fold		
Chris	Q♣6♦	fold		
Jerrod	8♦2♣	fold		
(Michelle)	A♠Q♠	re-raise to $15		
Nolan ($2 sb)	5♠2♠	fold		
Joan ($5 bb)	5♥3♦	fold		

Mick, under the gun with J♠T♦, raises to $10. Aaron folds, but Justin, getting annoyed with his trash hands, calls with A♣2♦. Mrs. Goldman, holding T♥7♠, is engrossed in a conversation with her husband and folds. Everyone else folds to Michelle, on the button with A♠Q♠, and she re-raises to $15; after all, Mick is a maniac. Nolan and Joan fold, while Mick and Justin call the re-raise. The pot's up to $48.

The flop comes T♠8♠9♥, giving Michelle the nut flush draw and a gutshot straight draw; Mick flops a straight draw and top pair. Mick bets his hand, and Justin angrily throws his cards into the muck. Michelle quickly raises with her draws to $10. Mick re-raises to $15, and Michelle caps it at $20. The pot is up to $88.

The turn is the K♦, helping neither player. Mick bets his pair of tens, and Michelle decides to just call. The pot is up to $108.

The river is the J♦, giving Michelle the nut straight and Mick two pair. Mick, not putting Michelle on the straight, decides to check-raise, and starts his plan by checking. Michelle bets of course, and Mick raises. Michelle looks back at her cards and verifies that she has the nuts before re-raising. Mick re-raises to $40. Michelle, realizing that Mick has the same hand, just calls. Mick turns over his cards, and says, "Two pair, baby! *Ship it!*" Michelle meekly turns over the nuts and takes down the $188 pot.

Analysis. One of the most important attributes of a poker player is patience. Justin doesn't have it, and his pre-flop calls were a waste of $15. A2o is *not* a hand worth calling one raise (let alone two) pre-flop from early position *even against a maniac.* Yes, Justin had position on the maniac, but nothing prevents another player from holding a premium hand. Michelle did, and Justin needlessly lost the $15.

The only other salient point is that Michelle should have kept raising on the river. When you have the nuts, it's the last round of betting, and you're heads-up, keep on betting. There's always a chance that you're facing someone who thinks he has the best hand but doesn't.

Chip Stacks: Mrs. Goldman $369; Peter: $58; Chris: $293; Jerrod: $293; Michelle: $378; Nolan: $616; Joan: $205; Mick: $198; Aaron: $500; Justin: $270

Before the next hand, Mick buys another $192 in chips. "I'm not going to be short in this game," he mumbles.

Hand 6.	Blinds $2/$5			
Players	Cards	Pre-Flop Action		
Aaron	A♥K♥	raise to $10	call $20 total	
Justin	9♥2♦	fold		
Mrs. Goldman	4♣4♦	call $10	call $20 total	
Peter	Q♠8♥	fold		
Chris	A♦J♣	re-raise to $15	call $20 total	
Jerrod	7♥6♥	fold		
Michelle	A♠K♠	re-raise to $20		
(Nolan)	J♠4♠	fold		
Joan ($2 sb)	K♦3♣	fold		
Mick ($5 bb)	J♦8♦	call $20		

Aaron is first to act and makes the raise to $10 with A♥K♥. Justin almost throws his cards at the dealer, then tosses his 9♥2♦ into the muck. Mrs. Goldman cold calls with 4♣4♦. Chris, seeing a big ace (A♦J♣), makes it three bets. Michelle caps the betting with A♠K♠. Mick calls with his suited J♦8♦. Mrs. Goldman and Chris also call the raises. The pot is $98 after the rake.

The flop comes T♦K♣2♣. Mick decides to check after thinking for a few moments. Even he realizes that his backdoor flush draw is no good. Aaron bets his top pair, top kicker. Mrs. Goldman calls, knowing she has two cards left to get her set. Chris calls with his gutshot straight draw and one overcard. Michelle decides to raise with her top pair/top kicker. Mick slides his cards into the muck. Aaron makes it three bets, and Mrs. Goldman quickly calls. Knowing Michelle is left to act behind him, and believing he's beat, Chris folds. Michelle just calls, fearing a possible set. The pot has grown to $148.

The turn is the Q♦, which would have given Chris the straight. Chris angrily smacks his hand on the padded rail. Aaron continues to bet. Mrs. Goldman calls the $10 bet, as does Michelle. The pot is now $178.

The river is the 8♣. Aaron bets, Mrs. Goldman sighs and folds, and Michelle just calls. They both turn over their ace-king hands and split the $198 pot.

Analysis. Chris's pre-flop raise is questionable. While AJo is a reasonable hand in late position in limit hold'em, he's facing an early position raise from a good player. It's likely that Aaron holds AA, KK, QQ, JJ, TT or AK. Chris's AJo doesn't look so good when you place it against Aaron's likely holding.

One day Mrs. Goldman will learn that small pocket pairs need a large field to get the correct odds. As we've said before, much of their value comes from flopping a set. If you play a small pocket pair against a raiser, and the flop contains two overcards (especially cards in the playing zone), it's time to cut your losses and fold. Here, Mrs. Goldman is playing a small pocket pair against *three* raisers and the flop not only has two overcards, it also contains a possible flush draw.

Chip Stacks: Mrs. Goldman $324; Peter: $58; Chris: $268; Jerrod: $293; Michelle: $422; Nolan: $616; Joan: $203; Mick: $370; Aaron: $544; Justin: $270

Hand 7.	Blinds $2/$5			
Players	Cards	Pre-Flop Action		
Justin	5♠2♣	call $5	call $10 total	
Mrs. Goldman	Q♦7♦	fold		
Peter	6♣6♦	call $5	call $10 total	
Chris	4♦3♦	fold		
Jerrod	A♥K♣	call $5	call $10 total	
Michelle	J♦4♣	fold		
Nolan	K♠Q♠	raise to $10		
(Joan)	T♠5♣	fold		
Mick ($2 sb)	9♣7♥	fold		
Aaron ($5 bb)	T♣2♥	fold		

Justin, under the gun with 5♠2♣, calls. He's bored. Mrs. Goldman, with Q♦7♦, decides to fold. She dislikes queen-high flush draws—it's a marginal hand. Peter elects to limp with 6♣6♦. Jerrod, holding A♥K♣, and seeing Peter in the hand, elects to just limp. Nolan, attempting to get the button, raises with K♠Q♠. Everyone else folds, and the limpers all call. The pot, after the rake, is $43.

The flop is J♠T♦8♠, giving Nolan both a flush draw and a straight draw. Justin checks, Peter checks, and Jerrod checks. Nolan bets, and Justin angrily folds (after muttering an obscenity). Peter, looking at the overcards, also folds. Jerrod calls. There's $53 in the pot.

The turn is the 3♠, giving Nolan the flush. Jerrod checks, Nolan bets $10, and Jerrod again calls. The pot is up to $73.

The river is the A♦, giving Jerrod top pair. Jerrod thinks for a moment, and has a bad feeling about the hand. He decides to just check and call. Nolan does indeed bet, and Jerrod calls. Nolan shows his flush and takes down the $93 pot.

Analysis. Jerrod should have raised with his AKo. You will not hold premium hands often during a session of hold'em, so you *must* make the most of them. Had Jerrod raised, it would not have changed the result of the hand (Nolan would have called or made it three bets with his K♠Q♠), but had Nolan held a more speculative hand such as K♠9♠, the raise could have made a difference. A case can also be made for Jerrod folding on the turn. Jerrod is facing a possible flush, and he is trailing a pair of deuces.

Chip Stacks: Mrs. Goldman $324; Peter: $48; Chris: $268; Jerrod: $258; Michelle: $422; Nolan: $674; Joan: $203; Mick: $368; Aaron: $539; Justin: $260

Hand 8.	Blinds $2/$5			
Players	Cards	Pre-Flop Action		
Mrs. Goldman	7♥4♣	call $5	call $15 total	call $20 total
Peter	Q♠4♠	fold		
Chris	9♥9♠	call $5	call $15 total	call $20 total
Jerrod	6♥5♣	fold		
Michelle	A♠8♠	call $5	call $15 total	call $20 total
Nolan	K♦T♠	call $5	fold	
Joan	A♣5♥	call $5	call $15 total	call $20 total
(Mick)	Q♥6♠	call $5	fold	
Aaron ($2 sb)	K♥K♣	raise to $10	re-raise to $20	
Justin ($5 bb)	K♠J♦	re-raise to $15	call $20 total	

Mrs. Goldman looks down at 7♥4♣. Knowing that she missed her straight when she held 74o the last time, she limps. Chris limps with 9♥9♠. Michelle decides to limp with A♠8♠. Nolan, seeing all the limpers and getting odds on his drawing hand, limps with K♦T♠. Joan, with A♣5♥, also limps. Mick decides to limp with Q♥6♠ because of all the callers. Aaron finds K♥K♣ in the small blind and raises to $10. Justin, still angry about his bad cards, decides to re-raise to $15 and then look at his cards (he holds K♠J♦). Mrs. Goldman calls the two additional bets. Chris calls and Michelle calls (she has an ace, after all), but Nolan folds. Joan calls, but Mick decides to fold. Aaron caps the betting, and everyone left in the hand calls. The pot is $126 after the $4 rake.

The flop is T♣4♦8♦, giving Mrs. Goldman bottom pair and Michelle middle pair. Aaron bets his overpair. Justin, looking at the huge pot, decides to call. Of course Mrs. Goldman calls with bottom pair. Chris and Michelle both call, each holding a pair. Joan decides to fold. The pot is now $151.

The turn is the J♣, giving Chris a straight draw and Justin top pair. Aaron again bets. Justin quickly and forcibly raises to $20. Mrs. Goldman has a pair so she calls. Chris also calls with his draw. Michelle decides to fold, figuring her pair is way behind. Aaron re-raises with his overpair, and Justin caps the betting. Mrs. Goldman and Chris both call. The pot has ballooned to $311.

The river is the 7♣, making a flush possible and giving Chris the straight. Aaron, fearing someone is on a flush draw, checks. Justin, having no fears, bets $10. Mrs. Goldman, who has made two pair, raises to $20. Chris immediately re-raises to $30. Aaron reluctantly folds, knowing that his one pair is beat by either Chris or Mrs. Goldman. Justin calls, as does Mrs. Goldman. Chris takes down the $401 pot.

Analysis. Note Aaron's actions on this hand. He pushed his hand whenever he could *until it was likely he was behind*. He then quietly folded his hand and got ready for the next hand. Yes, he was unlucky that his pair of kings didn't hold up but he realized that over time he would make money against this group of opponents.

Justin's impatience cost him again. Certainly his K♠J♦ was worth a *call* against this many players. However, when a solid player like Aaron raises, his hand is *not* worth a re-raise. Justin's bets on the river showed that he considered only his hand, not those of his opponents.

Chip Stacks: Mrs. Goldman $229; Peter: $48; Chris: $574; Jerrod: $258; Michelle: $397; Nolan: $669; Joan: $183; Mick: $363; Aaron: $474; Justin: $165

Hand 9.	Blinds $2/$5			
Players	Cards	Pre-Flop Action		
Peter	K♥2♥	fold		
Chris	8♣3♥	fold		
Jerrod	9♥9♠	call $5	call $10 total	
Michelle	J♥6♠	fold		
Nolan	6♦5♦	fold		
Joan	Q♦2♦	fold		
Mick	T♥3♣	raise to $10		
(Aaron)	9♦8♥	fold		
Justin ($2 sb)	K♦8♦	call $10 total		
Mrs. Goldman ($5 bb)	J♣9♣	call $10 total		

Jerrod limps with a pair of nines, 9♥9♠. Mick, seeing only one limper, raises with T♥3♣. Justin quickly calls with K♦8♦, as does Mrs. Goldman with J♣9♣ (her cards are suited, after all). Jerrod calls the raise. The pot is $36 after the rake.

The flop is J♠2♣4♣, giving Mrs. Goldman top pair and a flush draw. Justin checks, and Mrs. Goldman bets $5 on her flush draw (she hasn't noticed that she has top pair). Jerrod decides to call. Mick quickly raises with nothing. Justin shakes his head and folds. He also steps away from the table and yells something unpleasant at no one in particular. Mrs. Goldman just calls, worrying about a made hand, and Jerrod calls as well. The pot is now $66.

The turn is the Q♥. Mrs. Goldman checks, fearing Mick. Jerrod, fearing both players, checks. Mick continues his bluff and bets. Mrs. Goldman, still holding just a draw (in her mind), calls. Jerrod, seeing two overcards to his pair, folds. The pot is now $86.

The river is the 4♠. Mrs. Goldman checks, and Mick, knowing that Mrs. Goldman will call, decides to check. Mrs. Goldman says, "Jack high," and turns over her hand. Justin, back at the table, says, "You have two pair. Why weren't you betting?" The dealer pushes Mrs. Goldman the $86 as Mick mucks his hand.

Analysis. One day Mick will learn that bluffing against a calling station doesn't work. Until then, if you see Mick in a cardroom, try to get on his table. Justin was wrong to critique Mrs. Goldman's play at the table, but what he said was completely accurate.

Chip Stacks: Mrs. Goldman $285; Peter: $48; Chris: $574; Jerrod: $238; Michelle: $397; Nolan: $669; Joan: $183; Mick: $333; Aaron: $474; Justin: $155

Hand 10.	Blinds $2/$5			
Players	Cards	Pre-Flop Action		
Chris	K♦4♠	fold		
Jerrod	Q♦5♥	fold		
Michelle	A♠7♠	call $5	call $10 total	
Nolan	Q♥3♣	fold		
Joan	A♥8♠	call $5	call $10 total	
Mick	7♦5♠	raise to $10		
Aaron	9♦7♣	fold		
(Justin)	J♦8♣	fold		
Mrs. Goldman ($2 sb)	8♥2♠	fold		
Peter ($5 bb)	A♠Q♠	call $10 total		

Michelle limps with A♠7♠, as does Joan with A♥8♠. Mick raises with his 7♦5♠. Mrs. Goldman looks down at a hand that even she can fold without thinking, 8♥2♠, and does. Peter, in the big blind, just calls with his A♠Q♠. The limpers all call, and the pot is $38.

The flop is 5♣4♦A♦, giving Peter, Michelle, and Joan top pair. Peter decides to bet. Michelle calls, but Joan decides to raise with her ace. Mick, holding middle pair, makes it $15. Peter thinks about mucking his hand, but decides to call. Michelle calls. The pot has grown to $98.

The turn is the 4♥. Peter checks, Michelle checks, and Joan decides to check. Mick, knowing that someone has an ace, decides to also check. The pot remains at $98.

The river is the 9♥, and Peter still has the best hand, but he fears the worst, so he checks. Michelle, knowing she's beat, also checks. Joan bets, realizing that she's ahead of Mick based on his check on the turn, Mick decides to fold. Peter goes into the tank. After Justin threatens to call the floorman to have a clock put on Peter, he ever so reluctantly calls. Michelle folds. Joan turns over her hand, and Peter can't believe he's actually won the hand. He wins a $118 pot.

Analysis. If you hold middle pair, are facing a large group of limpers and an ace flops, you're most likely beat. The hand that most players will limp with is A*x*. Mick's raise was foolhardy. Additionally, Peter can't fear that monsters are always out against him. He would have won a larger pot had he raised pre-flop, raised on the flop, and bet the turn.

Chip Stacks: Mrs. Goldman $283; Peter: $131; Chris: $574; Jerrod: $238; Michelle: $372; Nolan: $669; Joan: $148; Mick: $308; Aaron: $474; Justin: $155

Wins and Losses in the Ten Limit Hold'em Hands:
Mrs. Goldman −$17; Peter +$31; Chris +$274; Jerrod -$62; Michelle +$72; Nolan +$169; Joan -$152; Mick -$184; Aaron -$26; and Justin -$145.

Justin, annoyed with his losses, tells everyone at the table, "Why don't we play a *real* game. Let's play some no-limit." Amazingly, no one objects. The floorman is brought over, and the game becomes a $1/$2 blind no-limit hold'em game with a $100 minimum and $300 maximum buy-in. Mrs. Goldman, Jerrod, Joan, and Justin rebuy to $300. The floorman brings cash for Chris, Michelle, Nolan, Mick, and Aaron so that their stacks are also at $300. Peter, though, elects to remain at a $131 stack because he is up for the day and that there's no reason to risk more.

Hands 11 – 20 (Ten No-Limit Hands)

Hand 11	Blinds $1/$2			
Players	Cards	Pre-Flop Action		
Jerrod	Q♣8♥	fold		
Michelle	8♣6♦	fold		
Nolan	A♣6♥	fold		
Joan	K♥K♦	raise to $20		
Mick	5♦3♦	call $20		
Aaron	3♥2♥	fold		
Justin	7♠6♣	fold		
(Mrs. Goldman)	9♦7♥	call $20		
Peter ($1 sb)	K♠J♣	fold		
Chris ($2 bb)	T♦8♦	call $20 total		

Joan is delighted to see K♥K♦, and raises to $20. Mick looks down at 5♦3♦ and calls. Mrs. Goldman sees 9♦7♥ and decides to call. She knows she can make a straight. Peter folds his K♠J♣ and Chris, holding T♦8♦, wants to show that he won't be pushed around in no-limit and he decides to also call. There's $77 in the pot going to the flop.

The flop is Q♦6♠2♠. Joan, fearing someone has a spade flush draw, bets $100. Mick thinks for a moment but decides that an inside straight draw and a backdoor flush draw aren't worth the call. Mrs. Goldman and Chris also muck, and Joan takes down the pot.

Analysis. Joan's pre-flop raise was too large. A raise to $12 (six times the big blind) would make the price wrong for callers. However, against *these* opponents, her raise might have been close to optimal. After all, she did get three callers. Of course, none of Joan's opponents should have called the pre-flop raise. Joan's flop bet was also too large. A pot-sized bet would still have given a caller the wrong price to draw.

Chip Stacks: Mrs. Goldman $280; Peter: $130; Chris: $280; Jerrod: $300; Michelle: $300; Nolan: $300; Joan: $357; Mick: $280; Aaron: $300; Justin: $300

Hand 12.	Blinds $1/$2			
Players	Cards	Pre-Flop Action		
Michelle	A♠6♥	call $2	call $12 total	
Nolan	5♠4♥	fold		
Joan	J♥2♠	fold		
Mick	A♦K♣	raise to $12		
Aaron	Q♥T♥	fold		
Justin	J♠8♠	call $12		
Mrs. Goldman	Q♣4♦	fold		
(Peter)	7♦5♦	fold		
Chris ($1 sb)	9♦9♥	call $12 total		
Jerrod ($2 bb)	T♦3♦	fold		

Michelle looks down at A♠6♥ and limps. Mick has a real hand, A♦K♣, and raises to $12. Justin looks down at J♠8♠ and decides to call with his position. Mrs. Goldman folds Q♣4♦. Peter also folds a trash hand, 7♦5♦. Chris, in the small blind, elects to call with pocket nines, 9♦9♥. Michelle, seeing that two players have called the raise, decides to call. There's $46 in the pot.

The flop comes T♣8♥K♦. Chris, seeing two overcards to his pair of nines, checks. Michelle also checks. Mick bets $30 with his top pair/top kicker. Justin flat calls with middle pair, knowing that Mick is a maniac. Chris and Michelle both fold. There's $106 in the pot going to the turn.

The turn is the 8♣. Mick bets $75 with his two pair. Justin, smiles, and makes the minimum raise to $150. Mick, having a real hand, gives it only a moment's hesitation and moves all-in for a total of $238. Justin calls. The players flip over their cards and Mick can't believe that Justin has outdrawn him. The river is the J♣, giving Justin a full house. Mick immediately rebuys for $300.

Analysis. Sometimes you can do everything right and still lose. And other times, you do everything wrong and win. Justin should never have called pre-flop, nor should he have called on the flop. But once he makes it to the turn, he's destined to win the hand. Mick gets very unlucky; this is a hand that Justin would have folded had he been up against a solid player such as Aaron or Nolan. Mick played the hand as he should (just like when he doesn't hold a hand).

Chip Stacks: Mrs. Goldman $280; Peter: $130; Chris: $268; Jerrod: $298; Michelle: $288; Nolan: $300; Joan: $357; Mick: $300; Aaron: $300; Justin: $602

Hand 13.	Blinds $1/$2		
Players	Cards	Pre-Flop Action	
Nolan	7♠4♦	folds	
Joan	A♥Q♣	raise to $20	call $268 total
Mick	Q♠5♦	fold	
Aaron	3♣2♦	fold	
Justin	3♥2♠	fold	
Mrs. Goldman	4♠4♣	call $20	fold
Peter	9♣6♥	fold	
(Chris)	K♠K♣	raise to $268	(all-in)
Jerrod ($1 sb)	9♥5♣	fold	
Michelle ($2 bb)	J♦9♠	fold	

Joan looks down at A♥Q♣ and raises to $20. Mrs. Goldman sees 4♠4♣ and makes the *easy* call. Chris looks down at his cards and spots K♠K♣ and begins to think. He decides to move all-in to protect his hand. So he has raised to a total of $268. After the blinds fold, it's back to Joan and she begins to think. She wonders if Chris has a middle pair like 10s or 9s, or a big hand like aces or kings. After thinking for a few moments, she decides to call. Mrs. Goldman wants to call, but even she realizes that she must be behind and folds. The players turn over their cards to battle for the $555 pot.

The flop comes A♠7♦7♥. The turn is the 8♦, and the river is the T♥ and Joan takes down the pot. Chris angrily reaches for his wallet and rebuys for $250.

Analysis. Once again, the worst hand wins. However, Chris should have lost a lot less money on this hand. Sure, Chris should have re-raised Joan. *But a re-raise to $80* would have been much more reasonable than a re-raise to $268. Chris *wants* Joan to call if she holds a hand like A♥Q♣. After all, Chris is a 72% favorite on the hand. If Chris had raised to $80 and Joan had called, it's likely that Chris would have been able to get away from his hand once the ace hits the board on the flop.

Chip Stacks: Mrs. Goldman $260; Peter: $130; Chris: $250; Jerrod: $297; Michelle: $286; Nolan: $300; Joan: $644; Mick: $300; Aaron: $300; Justin: $602

Hand 14.	Blinds $1/$2			
Players	Cards	Pre-Flop Action		
Joan	K♥6♦	call $2	call $4 total	
Mick	8♣2♥	fold		
Aaron	9♣6♠	fold		
Justin	A♠3♦	raise to $4		
Mrs. Goldman	7♦7♣	call $4		
Peter	T♠T♦	call $4		
Chris	J♠2♦	fold		
(Jerrod)	5♠2♠	fold		
Michelle ($1 sb)	9♦3♣	fold		
Nolan ($2 bb)	A♣Q♦	call $4 total		

Joan has K♥6♦ under the gun and limps. After all, she just won a big pot. Justin peers at A♠3♦ and raises to $4. Mrs. Goldman spots 7♦7♣ and makes the call. Peter looks down at T♠T♦ looks at his cards, looks at Justin, and then reluctantly calls. Everyone else folds to Nolan in the big blind. He spots A♣Q♦, and decides to only call because with this group of players he would get at least one call if he were to raise and he's going to be out of position the entire hand. Joan also calls, so the pot is $19 after $2 is taken for the rake.

The flop is Q♥K♦T♣, and almost everyone hits the flop except Mrs. Goldman and Justin. Nolan decides to bet $12 to find out where he is. Joan, holding top pair and fearing the straight, calls. Justin, now with only a straight draw, raises to $24. Mrs. Goldman thinks for a long time. She finally concludes that one of the players is ahead of her and she mucks her hand. Peter has a hard time believing he has flopped bottom set. He rechecks his cards, and he still has bottom set. Fearing the straight, he calls. Nolan, seeing all the money in the pot, has the right price and calls. Joan also calls. The pot is up to $113 as $2 more is taken for the rake.

The turn is the 8♦, putting a potential flush draw into the mixture. Nolan decides to check. Joan, who has a king, decides she's ahead and bets $100. Justin, still with just a straight draw, decides to fold. Peter goes into the tank. Eventually he comes to the conclusion that he can't muck a set, so he calls, leaving himself $2 for the river. Nolan decides to call, so the pot has grown to $413.

The river is the A♥. Nolan moves all-in for $172. Joan quickly calls, and Peter stops to think. He says, "What the hell," and throws in his $2. He's shocked when he takes down the main pot of $419. Nolan gets the side pot of $340.

Analysis. When we play no-limit hold'em, we frequently see players make the minimum possible raise. This is especially true in on-line games. Justin's raise to $4 is useless. Indeed, he should have folded his A3o. He's out of position with a weak ace; his minimum raise isn't going to scare anyone in *this* game.

Nolan's flop bet of $12 was excellent. He had a hand where he could be ahead or behind, and he needed to obtain information regarding where he stood. When two players call and one raises, Nolan knows he's *not* ahead.

Peter continues to fear the monsters. Peter should have re-raised on the flop. That's a very dangerous flop for a set, with three cards in the playing zone. If someone was drawing he needed to give him the wrong price to call. On the turn, Peter should have moved all-in for the additional $2. There was no reason to horde the $2 for a rainy day. Had he moved-in on the turn, he would have won an additional $2 (from Justin, who folded on the river).

On the turn, Nolan believed that Joan likely held only top pair. She *called* his bet on the flop and bet on the turn. Given her aggressiveness, Nolan felt that Joan would raise if she flopped a big hand such as a straight or a set. While it was possible Joan held K8o, it was much more likely she held some other Kx hand. Speaking of Joan, she should folded pre-flop. K6o is not a hand you want to play under the gun. Had she folded, she would have saved herself $300.

Chip Stacks: Mrs. Goldman $256; Peter: $419; Chris: $250; Jerrod: $297; Michelle: $285; Nolan: $340; Joan: $344; Mick: $300; Aaron: $300; Justin: $574

Hand 15.	Blinds $1/$2			
Players	Cards	Pre-Flop Action		
Mick	8♣2♥	fold		
Aaron	7♥2♦	fold		
Justin	K♣K♥	raise to $6	raise to $574	(all-in)
Mrs. Goldman	A♠A♥	call $6	call $256 total	(all-in)
Peter	9♣6♦	fold		
Chris	T♠8♥	fold		
Jerrod	9♦3♣	fold		
(Michelle)	Q♠Q♣	call $6	call $285 total	(all-in)
Nolan ($1 sb)	A♦A♣	raise to $50	call $340 total	(all-in)
Joan ($2 bb)	5♥2♣	fold		

Justin sees K♣K♥ and decides to raise to $6, as a raise to $4 didn't limit the field enough. Mrs. Goldman looks down at her cards, and can't believe she has A♠A♥. She decides to trap, so she just calls. It is folded to Michelle who looks down at Q♠Q♣ and decides to just call. Nolan looks down at A♦A♣ in the small blind and elects to raise to $50. Joan folds and the betting is back to Justin. Justin decides that now is the time to get his chips into the pot, so he moves all-in. Mrs. Goldman can't believe how well her trap has succeeded, and she also moves all-in. Michelle can't believe all the action that's happening. She also moves in, as does Nolan. The hands are revealed. There's $1,022 in the main pot that Mrs. Goldman is competing for. There's $87 in the side pot that Michelle, Nolan, and Justin are competing for, and $110 in the second side pot that Nolan and Justin are fighting over.

The flop is 7♠7♣2♠, and Aaron realizes he would have flopped a full house. The turn and river are the inconsequential 4♥ and 3♥. Nolan takes down both side pots, and Nolan and Mrs. Goldman split the main pot. Michelle rebuys for $300.

Analysis. Michelle should have considered what the other hands were rather than noticing all of the action. Had she gone through that exercise, she should have concluded that someone held AA or KK and been able to fold her queens. Pocket queens are a good hand, but aces and kings are better.

Chip Stacks: Mrs. Goldman $511; Peter: $419; Chris: $250; Jerrod: $297; Michelle: $300; Nolan: $708; Joan: $342; Mick: $300; Aaron: $300; Justin: $234

Hand 16.	Blinds $1/$2			
Players	Cards	Pre-Flop Action		
Aaron	K♠6♣	fold		
Justin	K♦5♣	fold		
Mrs. Goldman	8♣2♣	call $2	call $10 total	
Peter	J♠4♣	fold		
Chris	T♦7♦	fold		
Jerrod	Q♦T♠	call $2	fold	
Michelle	Q♥5♠	fold		
(Nolan)	T♣2♥	fold		
Joan ($1 sb)	7♥2♦	raise to $10		
Mick ($2 bb)	7♠3♦	fold		

Mrs. Goldman elects to call with her suited hand, 8♣2♣. Jerrod reluctantly calls with Q♦T♠. Joan looks down at her favorite hand, the hammer, 7♥2♦, and raises to $10. Mrs. Goldman calls but Jerrod folds. There's $20 in the pot after the house takes $2 for the rake.

The flop is 5♦9♥8♦, giving Mrs. Goldman middle pair. Joan decides to make a teaser bet of $5. Mrs. Goldman quickly calls. There's $29 in the pot after the house takes another $1 for the rake.

The turn is the 2♠. Joan, now holding a pair, decides to make a real bet, and bets $10. Mrs. Goldman again quickly calls. She hasn't noticed that she has two pair, and thinks that all she has is a pair of eights. There's $48 in the pot after $1 more is taken for the rake.

The river is the 3♠. Joan figures that a check is probably best, as it appears Mrs. Goldman would call any bet and all she has is a pair of deuces. Mrs. Goldman, thinking that she has just a pair of eights, also checks, and she takes the pot with her two pair.

Analysis. Joan may have been able to bet a player off their hand. However, if she had been paying attention to how Mrs. Goldman had been playing her hands, once she called on the flop it's likely that she held either a flush draw or a pair and would be calling until the river. Of course, Joan should have just folded pre-flop. Again, had Mrs. Goldman correctly read her hand, she would have taken down a larger pot.

Chip Stacks: Mrs. Goldman $534; Peter: $419; Chris: $250; Jerrod: $297; Michelle: $300; Nolan: $708; Joan: $317; Mick: $298; Aaron: $300; Justin: $234

Hand 17.	Blinds $1/$2			
Players	Cards	Pre-Flop Action		
Justin	A♦J♦	raise to $30		
Mrs. Goldman	5♠5♦	fold		
Peter	K♦J♣	fold		
Chris	T♦3♥	fold		
Jerrod	9♠6♣	fold		
Michelle	Q♣J♠	fold		
Nolan	A♣3♠	fold		
(Joan)	T♥8♣	fold		
Mick ($1 sb)	T♠8♦	fold		
Aaron ($2 bb)	K♠4♥	fold		

Justin looks down at A♦J♦ and raises to $30. Mrs. Goldman looks down at 5♠5♦, and angrily glares at Justin, and folds. Everyone else quickly folds. Justin picks up the $3 in blinds.

Analysis. Blind stealing in no-limit hold'em when the blinds are very small (as they were in this game) is not a profitable strategy. You want to raise and have your opponents make bad calls against you. Here, Justin's large raise to $30 ensures that he will either get *no* callers or be called by someone who holds a better hand than him.

In a game with a line-up like this, it's wise to raise a *normal* amount with your premium hands (in this case, about five to six times the big blind would be sufficient). You want players like Mrs. Goldman, Michelle, and Mick calling your raises with inferior speculative hands. Sure, once in a while they will wake up with a real hand, or they'll call and draw out on you, but in the long run you will make much more money giving your opponents the opportunity to make loose calls.

Chip Stacks: Mrs. Goldman $534; Peter: $419; Chris: $250; Jerrod: $297; Michelle: $300; Nolan: $708; Joan: $317; Mick: $297; Aaron: $298; Justin: $237

Hand 18.	Blinds $1/$2			
Players	Cards	Pre-Flop Action		
Mrs. Goldman	J♥3♦	fold		
Peter	9♠9♣	call $2	fold	
Chris	6♦3♥	fold		
Jerrod	K♥K♦	raise to $20		
Michelle	9♦4♦	fold		
Nolan	A♠Q♥	fold		
Joan	7♥7♣	call $20		
(Mick)	6♠4♠	fold		
Aaron ($1 sb)	Q♠9♥	fold		
Justin ($2 bb)	8♦5♥	fold		

Peter, holding 9♠9♣, limps. Jerrod looks down at K♥K♦ and begins to think. He raises to $20. Michelle folds, and Nolan looks down at A♠Q♥, realizes that Jerrod is the raiser, and quickly folds. Joan sees 7♥7♣ and makes the easy call (easy in her mind, at least). Everyone else folds. Peter looks forlorn at his 9♠9♣ and tosses them into the muck. The pot is $41 after the rake.

The flop comes 2♠Q♣J♦. Jerrod decides to check and trap Joan. Joan bets $2. Jerrod raises to $10. Joan, knowing that she's beat, folds. Jerrod takes down the pot.

Analysis. Nolan made a fold with a hand (A♠Q♥) that is worth a raise against some players. But when a tight player like Jerrod raised, Nolan knew that he was behind *and that he didn't have the correct price to call.* Notice also Joan's pre-flop call and Peter's pre-flop limp and fold. Peter correctly read Jerrod for either a big ace (in which case it's a coin-toss hand) or a big pair (in which case Peter is substantially behind). Joan's call with pocket sevens of a raise to $20 is wrong in a heads-up situation. Joan must call $20 to win a pot of $25. Since her expected return on the pot is 19.5%, she needs the pot to lay her 4.1 to 1 in order to make the call. Even when you consider implied pot odds Joan doesn't have the correct price to call.

Chip Stacks: Mrs. Goldman $534; Peter: $417; Chris: $250; Jerrod: $320; Michelle: $300; Nolan: $708; Joan: $295; Mick: $297; Aaron: $297; Justin: $235

Hand 19.	Blinds $1/$2			
Players	Cards	Pre-Flop Action		
Peter	Q♥Q♣	fold		
Chris	8♥5♠	fold		
Jerrod	7♠4♥	fold		
Michelle	J♣2♦	fold		
Nolan	8♣8♠	raise to $12		
Joan	Q♦3♣	fold		
Mick	K♠J♦	call $12		
(Aaron)	7♥7♣	call $12		
Justin ($1 sb)	A♣5♥	call $12 total		
Mrs. Goldman ($2 bb)	K♣2♣	call $12 total		

Peter is under the gun and spots one of his least favorite hands, Q♥Q♣. He decides it's too risky to play that hand in early position and mucks. Nolan looks down at 8♣8♠, and decides to raise to $12. Joan folds, but Mick decides to see a flop with K♠J♦. Aaron, Justin, and Mrs. Goldman decide to call. The pot is $56 after the rake is taken.

The flop comes Q♠9♣3♦. Justin decides to see what's going on and checks. Mrs. Goldman sees that she has a backdoor flush draw and bets $3. Nolan, unable to figure where he stands, but getting almost 20 to 1 odds, calls. Mick, with an inside straight draw, calls. Aaron, also getting great odds, calls. Justin figures that he, too, has the right price, so he also calls. The pot is up to $71.

The turn is the 4♦, putting a possible flush draw out and giving Justin a wheel draw. Justin decides to check. Mrs. Goldman, seeing that her hand didn't improve, also checks. Nolan thinks he may have the best hand and decides to make an almost pot-sized bet of $60. Mick thinks Nolan is on a steal, and makes it $120. Aaron, with only a pair of sevens, folds. Justin and Mrs. Goldman quickly fold. Nolan realizes he's likely behind and he'd have to make a huge call on the river to find out if he were ahead. So he folds. Mick takes down the $251 pot.

Analysis. Peter feared monsters yet again. Peter lost out on a big pot again.

This is the kind of hand where an aggressive player like Mick shines. Nolan knows that Mick will play any two cards. It's entirely possible that he has Q9 or even 43. Nolan, holding just a pair of eights, is out of position to Mick and could easily be trailing him. Mick is able to bet Nolan off the hand, and on this hand Mick's aggression pays off.

Chip Stacks: Mrs. Goldman $519; Peter: $417; Chris: $250; Jerrod: $320; Michelle: $300; Nolan: $633; Joan: $295; Mick: $413; Aaron: $282; Justin: $220

Hand 20.	Blinds $1/$2			
Players	Cards	Pre-Flop Action		
Chris	9♠6♦	fold		
Jerrod	4♠4♦	call $2	call $6 total	
Michelle	A♣T♣	raise to $4	call $6 total	
Nolan	7♥7♣	call $4	call $6 total	
Joan	A♠6♠	call $4	call $6 total	
Mick	K♥Q♥	call $4	call $6 total	
Aaron	J♦J♣	call $4	call $6 total	
(Justin)	K♠T♠	call $4	call $6 total	
Mrs. Goldman ($1 sb)	Q♦Q♣	re-raise to $6		
Peter ($2 bb)	3♥3♦	call $6		

Jerrod limps with his pocket pair, but Michelle has A♣T♣ and raises to $4. Nolan has 7♥7♣ and calls the $4. Joan and Mick call with their speculative hands. Aaron has J♦J♣ and thinks that someone is slow-playing a big hand so he, too, just calls. Justin has K♠T♠ and decides to play along. Mrs. Goldman, in the small blind, sees a pair of queens. She realizes that she hasn't been very aggressive, so she re-raises to $6. Peter spots pocket 3s and decides to call. Everyone else also just calls. The pot is $50 going to the flop.

The flop comes Q♠2♠T♥. Mrs. Goldman realizes that she has the best possible hand. Not to appear weak, she follows up her pre-flop re-raise with a bet of $2. Peter decides to fold his pocket 3s. Jerrod folds his pocket 4s. Michelle, with middle pair, top kicker, calls. Nolan, with a pair, and odds of almost 30 to 1, calls. Joan, with the nut flush draw, decides to raise to $10. Mick, holding top pair, good kicker, and a backdoor flush draw, calls. Aaron, with his jacks, calls. Justin, with his flush draw, calls. Mrs. Goldman, after trying to raise to $12, decides to call instead. Michelle and Nolan call. The pot is up to $120.

The turn is the A♥, giving Michelle two pair and Mick a nut flush draw. Mrs. Goldman, still holding what she thinks is the best hand, decides to make a big bet and bets $10. Michelle, with her two pair, and a very scary board, elects to call. Nolan knows he's way behind and folds his sevens. Joan, with top pair, and a nut flush draw, decides to call. Mick, now with a bunch of draws and a pair of queens, raises to $75. Aaron, figures he must behind at least two players, decides to fold. Justin with what he thinks is a great flush draw, happily calls. Mrs. Goldman quickly calls, as do Michelle and Joan. The pot has ballooned to $495.

The river is the J♠, giving Joan the nut flush, Justin the second nut flush, and Mick top straight. Mrs. Goldman can't figure out what's going on, and decides to check. Michelle, hating the river, also checks. Joan, holding the nuts, moves all-in for $204. Mick, with his straight, decides he has the best hand, and moves all-in for $322. Justin, with his flush, knows there's a slight chance he may be beat, but getting almost 8 to 1, knows he must call. So he moves all-in for $129. Mrs. Goldman decides to work out the hand. After attempting to do so for two minutes, she shakes her head, and says, "I don't see how I can get away from this hand," and she calls $322. Michelle knows she's beat and folds. The main pot is $1,011; the first side pot, which Joan, Mick, and Mrs. Goldman are in, totals $225. The second side pot, between Mick and Mrs. Goldman, has the remaining $236. Joan takes down the main pot and the first side pot while Mick takes down the second side pot.

Analysis. Mrs. Goldman throws down her cards, looks at the board and at all the money in the pot, and stammers, "I can't believe you people play almost any two cards. You're just a bunch of … *palookas!*" Well, perhaps Mrs. Goldman's poker tutor will teach her about bet sizes in no-limit hold'em. Her $2 pre-flop re-raise isn't going to get anyone out of the pot; she should have made a substantial re-raise, to *at least* $30. Had she done so, she might have faced only Mick and Aaron. In a three-way hand with the flop of Q♠2♠T♥, she should have made a substantial bet. With a flush draw out against her and a possible straight draw, even moving all-in would be reasonable. It's impossible to judge whether she would have won the pot had she done so (Mick, being a maniac, *might* have called) but it's probable that she would have. Given her actions, she made certain that she would lose this pot.

Final Chip Stacks: Mrs. Goldman $106; Peter: $411; Chris: $250; Jerrod: $314; Michelle: $209; Nolan: $617; Joan: $1,236; Mick: $236; Aaron: $266; Justin: $0

Wins and Losses in the Ten No-Limit Hands: Mrs. Goldman, -$194; Peter, +$280; Chris, -$300; Jerrod, +$14; Michelle, -$391; Nolan, +$317; Joan, +$936; Mick, -$364; Aaron, -$34; and Justin, -$300

Overall Wins and Losses: Mrs. Goldman, -$211; Peter, +$311; Chris, -$26; Jerrod, -$48; Michelle, -$319; Nolan, +$486; Joan, +$784; Mick, -$548; Aaron, -$60; and Justin, -$445.

Analysis and Conclusions

We thought of an interesting experiment. What if we replaced *one* player at the table with a good (but not great) player who would make reasonable plays? What would the impact be for each of our players? (We'll skip this experiment for our two good players, Nolan and Aaron.)

Mrs. Goldman. Our substitute folds Hand 1. He won't get involved with 65o facing two raises (-$113). On Hand 2, we'll let her actions stand. While it would be reasonable to fold pre-flop, calling until the river is also acceptable. On Hand 3, our substitute quickly folds and saves $30. He won't get involved with pocket 3s facing two raises. On Hand 4, the substitute folds and won't make the magical flush (-$26). No change on Hand 5. On Hand 6, pocket fours in early position don't interest the substitute and he saves $45. No change on Hand 7. Our sub would quickly fold 74o on Hand 8, saving $95. On Hand 9, our substitute would win more money than Mrs. Goldman did. Her call is correct pre-flop with her one-gap suited connectors. The substitute would either raise on the flop or turn and would certainly bet the river. We'll say that the sub would have won, conservatively, an additional $20. No change on Hand 10. So for the limit hold'em hands, our substitute would have had $51 more (for a profit of $34 instead of a loss of $17).

On Hand 11, our substitute would fold 97o to a $20 raise. On Hand 12, no change. On Hand 13, no pre-flop call so our substitute saves another $20. No change on Hands 14 and 15. On Hand 16, our substitute would fold to the raise (-$23). No change on Hands 17 and 18. On Hand 19, our substitute would fold K2s out of position, saving $10. Hand 20 is more difficult to determine. Our substitute would certainly make a big raise, limiting the field. Depending on the size of the raise, and the flop betting, he would get heads-up with Aaron, winning a big pot (set over set on the river). Some of the time, though, Mick will call (after all, he's a maniac). Mrs. Goldman lost $308 on the hand as played; we'll estimate that she would win $308 half the time and lose $308 half the time, for an expected result of $0. This is a savings of $308. But we think you would agree that a reasonable player would *not* play Hand 20 in the same manner that Mrs. Goldman did. So, on the ten no-limit hands, our substitute would do $335 better than Mrs. Goldman did; overall, he'd do $386 better.

Peter. No change on Hands 1 and 2. On Hand 3, a reasonable player would have *lost* more money than Peter did. He would re-raise pre-flop and would certainly bet and raise more post-flop. We'll estimate that he would lose $35 more. No change on Hands 4 through 9. On Hand 10, a decent player would re-raise with AQs in the big blind and would certainly bet on the turn and river. We'll estimate that Peter would have won an additional $50, $15 from the re-raise pre-flop, $15 from a re-raise on the flop, and $20 from a bet on the turn. Overall, our substitute would win $15 more in the limit hold'em hands.

No change on Hands 11 through 13. On Hand 14, Peter could have won an additional $2 by moving all-in on the turn, but we'll ignore that for this analysis. Certainly our reasonable player would get his money all-in with his set. Additionally, our substitute would likely have bought in for the *maximum* possible ($300) for the no-limit session, rather than staying at $131. This, too, would have increased his winnings. But we'll ignore that, too. No change on Hands 15 through 18. On Hand 19, our substitute would make a raise, say to $12. We'll assume that Mick and Mrs. Goldman would call. The substitute would flop a set, bet out, and would likely take down the pot. We'll estimate conservatively that he would have won $25. No change on Hand 20. So our substitute would win at least $25 more in the no-limit hands, for an overall gain of $40.

Chris. No change on Hands 1 through 5. On Hand 6, our substitute would fold his AJo to Aaron's under the gun raise, saving $25. No change on Hands 7 or 8 (Chris played this hand quite well). No change on Hands 9 or 10. The substitute would earn an additional $25 in the limit round.

Our substitute would fold Hand 11. While Chris' idea of not being pushed around is good, T8s isn't the hand to defend with (savings of $20). No change on Hands 12 or 13. On Hand 13, Chris got his money in with the best of it but was unlucky and lost. No change on Hands 14 through 20, making the net savings on the no-limit hands $20, and the overall savings $45.

Jerrod. No change on Hands 1 through 6. On Hand 7, our reasonable player would make a pre-flop raise with AKo. Most of the time, Nolan would call the two bets. The end result would either be the same (check calling on the river) or a savings of two big bets by folding on the turn. We'll estimate a savings of $10. No change on Hand 8. On Hand 9, the reasonable player would either fold on the flop or the turn (where Jerrod folded). We'll say that there's no change here. No change on Hand 10. The substitute would save $10 in the limit hold'em hands.

On Hands 11 through 15, no change. On Hand 16, it's possible that the substitute would raise, costing $10, or fold, saving $2, or make the same actions as Jerrod. We'll put the hand down as a loss of $5 (somewhere in the middle). No change on Hand 17. On Hand 18, if our substitute makes the de facto raise to $12, it's possible he'll get a call from someone other than Joan and win a larger pot. We'll conservatively estimate this as no change. No change on Hands 19 and 20. So the reasonable player has an average loss of $5 in the no-limit hands, for a net gain of $5.

Michelle. On Hand 1, our substitute folds without thinking. He won't play J7s from second position. That saves $15. No change on Hands 2 and 3. On Hand 4, our substitute would fold Q6o from the small blind. He doesn't feel that 5 to 1 on his money is good enough with a trash hand out of position. This will save $3. On Hand 5, our reasonable player would keep raising on the river, netting *at least* an additional $10. No change on Hands 6 or 7. On Hand 8, our substitute would either fold pre-flop (for no bets or one bet), or on the flop. We'll again be conservative and assume a fold on the flop, saving only $5. No change on Hand 9. The substitute folds Hand 10 without thinking. A7s in early/middle position is not a hand you want to play. This saves $25. The overall extra money for the limit hold'em hands is $58.

No change on Hand 11. Our reasonable player folds A6o on Hand 12 under the gun, saving $12. No change on Hands 13 or 14. On Hand 15, our reasonable player would not assume that Justin, Mrs. Goldman, or Nolan (still left to act behind him) has aces or kings. In fact, he would re-raise from $6 to $30 when the action got to him. It's likely that Nolan would have re-raised to $75, and Justin would have moved all-in and Mrs. Goldman would have called. The substitute would *then* know that *at least* one opponent held kings or aces and would now fold. We'll call this hand a savings of $261. No change on Hands 16 through 20. On Hand 20, Michelle's actions given the betting were reasonable. Thus, our substitute would save $273 in the no-limit hands, for an overall savings of $331.

Joan. On Hand 1, our reasonable player would either fold the hand pre-flop or play the hand exactly as Joan did. We'll be conservative with the savings and say that the substitute played Hand 1 as Joan did. But our substitute would quickly fold Hand 2 to a raise from Nolan, saving $30. Likewise, the reasonable player would fold the suited connectors (87s) on Hand 3, saving $15. The substitute wouldn't dream of playing A8o from under the gun on Hand 4 for a savings of $20. No change on Hands 5 through 7. On Hand 8, Joan's initial limp is reasonable (with her A5o in late position), but our substitute would fold to the raise and re-raise pre-flop, saving $10. No change on Hand 9. On Hand 10, our substitute would fold pre flop, saving $35. Overall, the substitute would save $110 in the limit hold'em hands.

On Hand 11, our substitute would make a smaller pre-flop raise (to $12), and would make a smaller bet on the flop (say $30). In this case, this would likely cost $16 in lost winnings (though it would, in the long run, have a better chance of getting a call from a player who shouldn't call). No change on Hand 12. On Hand 13, the substitute would make a smaller pre-flop raise, and Chris would either *call* or re-raise. Given that Mrs. Goldman would call a smaller re-raise, it's likely that the substitute would get the right price to continue with the hand and then get quite lucky on the flop. But in the interest of being conservative, we'll assume that our substitute would still face an all-in re-raise and would fold (cost of $287). On Hand 14, our reasonable player would fold pre-flop, saving $300. No change on Hand 15. On Hand 16, we'll assume that the substitute would *limp* pre-flop and would check and/or fold on the flop (he won't bet with his 72o), leading to a savings of $25. No change on Hand 17. On Hand 18, the reasonable player would fold pre-flop, saving $22. No change on Hands 19 and 20. For the no-limit hands, our reasonable player would save $44, for an overall savings of $154.

Mick. On Hand 1, our substitute folds, saving $55. On Hand 2, our substitute folds to Nolan's raise and saves $50. No change on Hands 3 and 4. The reasonable player would fold JTo under the gun on Hand 5, saving $85. On Hand 6, our substitute would fold pre-flop, saving another $20. No change on Hands 7 and 8. Given the number of limpers, and Mick's position on the button, his limp wasn't that bad of a play. His fold to the two additional bets was wise. But our substitute would fold pre-flop on Hand 9, saving $30. Nor would he raise on Hand 10; instead, he would fold, saving another $25. The savings from the limit hold'em hands stands at $265.

On Hand 11, our substitute would fold, saving $20. In a very deep-stack game, making calls with 53s can pay off; however, in a restricted buy-in game you're throwing money away when you call with trash hands. No change on Hand 12; Mick got unlucky on that hand and we'll assume the same misfortune falls on our substitute. No change on Hands 13 through 18. On Hand 19, Mick made a good, aggressive play that we'll assume the substitute doesn't find; that costs $116. On Hand 20, given the betting, our substitute would call *until the river*. Then, though, he would fold, figuring that *at least* one of his opponents made the flush. That would save $322, for an overall savings on the no-limit hands of $226, and a total savings of $491.

Justin. On Hand 1, no change. Justin's call in position isn't that bad and we're precluding brilliant plays from our substitute. No change on Hands 2 through 4. Our substitute quietly folds Hand 5, saving $15. No change on Hand 6. On Hand 7, the reasonable player folds 52o under the gun, saving $10. On Hand 8, our substitute folds his KJo to a raise from a good player, saving another $95. On Hand 9, the substitute quietly folds to the pre-flop raise, saving $8. No change on Hand 10. The net savings on the limit hold'em hands is $128.

No change on Hand 11. On Hand 12, our substitute folds J8s to a pre-flop raise. Here, that move costs $302 but it is the long-term winning play. No change on Hand 13. On Hand 14, our substitute wouldn't make the raise to $4; indeed, he would fold, saving $28. Hand 15 is more problematic. The substitute will make a reasonable raise, say to $12. Mrs. Goldman will call, Michelle will call, and Nolan will re-raise to $60. Now, the substitute will re-raise to $160. Mrs. Goldman and Michelle will again call, and Nolan will move all-in. Will the substitute get away from kings? It's possible, but not probable. If the substitute pauses and watches Mrs. Goldman, he will, because it's almost certain that Mrs. Goldman will give away her hand. But we're precluding our substitute from brilliancies, so we'll estimate that 25% of the time the substitute will get away from his kings, losing only $160 instead of $340. That's an estimated savings of $45. No change on Hand 16. On Hand 17, our substitute will make a normal raise to $12, and Mrs. Goldman will call. We'll assume that the substitute wins a $50 pot, quite reasonable given Mrs. Goldman, for a net gain of $27. No change on Hand 18. The substitute folds Hand 19, saving $15. Hand 20 is also difficult to determine. The substitute would certainly call pre-flop. The flop is so good that he would likely re-raise (say to $40) to find out where he stood. It becomes almost impossible to figure out what would happen. Certainly Mrs. Goldman would at least call. Joan might re-raise with her nut flush draw. Some of the time the betting would convince the substitute that he's facing a monster, and that he would not have the right price. We'll estimate that at 25% of the time, and that he would save $174. Most of the time, the money would move all-in somewhere in the betting. Still, the expected savings on this hand is $43 (rounded down from $43.50). That gives the substitute a *worse* result in the no-limit hands by $144, and an overall worse result of $16. We do point out that this is because of *one* hand that was played correctly by the substitute and *incorrectly* by Justin.

Interestingly enough, in almost every case the substitute did better than the original player. The substitute did *not* do anything brilliant. He just played good, solid poker and improved upon the results of almost all the players. If not for a very lucky card, he would have improved on the results of *all* the players.[47] This just shows you how much money the average player throws away playing poker today.

---

[47]It may be that the authors were unable to construct a series of hands without having one of the suboptimal tacticians having better results than a reasonable player would.

This concludes our views on why you lose at poker. You will agree with some of them, and maybe disagree with others. And that's how it should be. If you accept every word of this text as the truth without verifying it yourself (the easiest way to do so is just observe some games), you're losing the value of the book.

Play *your* style of poker. No matter what the "experts" say, there is no *one* right way of playing. If you're tight, stay tight, and try to channel some aggression into your game when you play your few hands. If you're loose, begin to throw away some of your uglier holdings and play loose and aggressive when you have position. Experiment if you can in some of the very low limit games to see what suits you.

So take from this book what you like and agree with. Don't ignore the points you disagree with; rather, determine why you think they're wrong (or don't apply to your games). Have fun at the tables and remember the overall goal of playing poker—making money.

Appendices

Pot Odds and Variance

Pot Odds

Understanding pot odds is simple. The most basic definition would be *the ratio between the money in the pot and the money it costs you to call the bet.* Simply stated, *pot odds* is the price the pot is laying you to make a call.

For example, if there is $50 in the pot and it will cost you $10 to call, the pot is laying you $50 to $10, more commonly notated as 5 to 1 (or simply 5:1). Similarly, if there is $180 in the pot and the price to call is $60, you are getting 3 to 1 on your call. If the pot is $300 and it is $5 to call (a very rare situation), you are getting 60 to 1.

But what do you do with pot odds? How is it useful? Glad you asked.

Let's say you're playing in a $3-$6 hold'em game. You hold A♦3♦ and the flop is J♦9♠6♦. There are five players in the hand, and you are last to act. With five players seeing the flop, they've each put $3 into the pot, making the total pot $15. On the flop, the first player has bet and two of the other three players have called, and it's up to you. There is $24 in the pot and it's going to cost you $3 to call and go for that flush. Do you call?

Before you answer that question, you're going to need a little bit more information. For example, what are the odds of you making your flush with two more cards to come when you already have four of that suit? Avoiding decimals, it's pretty safe to estimate that the odds are 2 to 1 against you making the flush. So, if the pot is laying you better than 2 to 1 odds, you can call.

In this example, with $24 in the pot and only a $3 call to you, the pot is laying you 8:1, and those odds are way more than enough to call and go for the flush. It's an easy call (and there's also a case for raising, but that play is beyond the scope of this appendix).

So you make the call. Now let's say the turn card does not bring your flush. The first player has bet $6, but the second player has raised to $12. Everyone has folded to you, and you have to decide whether to call or fold. On the flop, there was $27 in the pot after your call. Now there is $45 in the pot after the bet and raise, and it's going to cost you $12 to cold-call the raise. Do you call?

Well, you're now about a 4 to 1 underdog to make your flush with one card to come, so you'll need at least 4:1 odds from the pot to make this call. The pot is laying you $45:$12, or 3.75 to 1. Not very good. And with the threat of a possible re-raise (or two) behind you, you should fold your hand in this spot.

With the mention of possible raises behind you, we'll briefly discuss a concept called implied odds. This is more of an advanced topic, but one you should be at least vaguely familiar with. The theory of *implied odds* simply states that you need to sometimes take future bets into consideration when you are making a call (or raise). Sometimes these future bets can be enough to turn a fold into a call. For example, if you are getting only 3:1 from the pot, but there are 5 players left to act behind you, you might actually be getting as much as 8:1 from the pot if they all call. *However*, implied odds can also work in the opposite direction.

Suppose some of these players behind you are aggressive and might raise or even re-raise after you've called with proper odds? The concept of future raises such as this is called *reverse implied odds*. Reverse implied odds come into play when it is most likely going to cost you more to chase your draws than might be apparent. This can make an obvious call become a folding situation.

For now, you need only be concerned with pot odds. They are a very important tool to have in your poker toolbox, and they can quite often be the deciding factor in the play of a poker hand.

A Word about Variance

If you play poker for any length of time, you will hear the word *variance*. It's mentioned in almost every poker book, usually with a negative connotation. Yet once you understand variance you will realize that this concept keeps poor players coming back to the tables and helps to pad your pockets with their money.

The dictionary defines variance as "A difference between what is expected and what actually occurs."[48] Let's look at a practical example. Assume you toss a fair coin 1,000 times, and see how many times "heads" comes up. You do this experiment five times and heads comes up 487, 532, 449, 599, and 504 times. Each of these experimental results shows variance from the expected result of 500.

Now lets translate this to a poker example. Assume that Nolan is a winning player in $15-$30 limit hold'em. Over the last three years, he's played over a thousand hours of this game, with a win rate of $40/hour. Today Nolan played six hours of $15-$30 hold'em, and he ended up making a profit of $120. What is Nolan's variance?

From a poker standpoint, Nolan expected to make $40/hour × 6 hours = $240. He made $120, so he had a negative variance of $120.[49]

We can see variance in almost every aspect of poker. Let's say that you have A♠A♣ and you're all-in pre-flop against K♠K♣. Most of the time, you're going to win the hand. When you lose, we call it a *bad beat* or a *statistical anomaly*. This is another example of a negative variance.

Yet without variance, the bad players would soon stop playing. Assume the rules of poker changed and that it was played more like "War," the card game we played as kids. If you had a dominated hand, you *automatically* lost—no drawing out for the bad beat against your opponent. The poor players would quickly learn that they couldn't win. They'd be up against players holding the nuts.

Luckily, poker is a form of gambling. Sometimes the bad players win. They taste victory and have a desire to come back to the tables. The *positive variance* that they've experienced reinforces bad behavior. A few of these players will take the steps needed to learn how to become long-term winning players, although most will con-

---

[48]From http://www.dictionary.com; The American Heritage Dictionary of the English Language, Fourth Edition.

[49]From a statistical standpoint, this is *not* variance; rather, it is a *sample deviation from the mean*. In statistics, variance is defined as the *square* of the standard deviation. When you square any number (negative or positive), the result is a positive number (e.g. $(-7)^2 = 49$). Statistically, there is no such thing as a negative variance. In the poker world, almost everyone says "variance" when they really mean the statistical sample deviation from the mean.

tinue to be overall losing players with a winning session thrown in from time-to-time.

Casinos are built this way. The house advantage in most casino games is quite small—typically two to three percent.[50] Yet Las Vegas has grand palaces dedicated to gaming, testimony to the fact that over time, and with a huge volume of players, the house makes quite a bit of money with just a small edge. There are winners in every game, of course, and even though the *average* or *mean* result is a loss, some players will have a "good day" on occasion. This is *positive variance* by breaking even or winning.

So don't fear variance. Welcome it. But be prepared for it. Make sure you have the proper bankroll (see Chapter 10, *Losing Because You Don't Have an Adequate Bankroll*, beginning on page 83) so you're ready to cover the swings that are guaranteed to happen. Yes, variance will cause you to have days at the tables you would rather forget, but it will also cause the poor players to have good days that will lead them to play again.

---

[50]There are a few casino games where the house has a tremendous edge, such as Keno. In Keno, the house usually will have a 25% - 30% advantage on bets.

♠ *APPENDIX B* ♥

Further Reading

In the past two years, the number of poker books has increased dramatically. There's even a poker section at our local bookstore. Our goal with this list is to be able to whet your appetite for some good books well worth purchasing. All of the books and most of the software mentioned here can be purchased at bookstores specializing in poker and gambling, including the online store at ConJelCo (www.conjelco.com).

We started writing this book by reading (or re-reading, in the case of the one of us who is a bridge player) a classic bridge book, *Why You Lose at Bridge.* This book, by S. J. Simon, has been in print for sixty years. If you're a bridge player, buy it and read it. It *will* help your game.

If you're going to play seven-card stud, Roy West's book, *Seven-Card Stud: A Complete Course in Winning at Medium and Lower Limits*, is a great introduction to the game. There's also plenty of sage advice on poker in general within the pages of West's book.

Regrettably, there have been few good books written on split-pot games. Ray Zee's *High-Low-Split Poker Seven-Card Stud and Omaha Eight-or-Better for Advanced Players*, is the best book written on the subject. It's a bit weighty, though. A good introduction to Omaha high/low is Mark Tenner and Lou Krieger's *Winning Omaha 8 Poker.*

Gary Carson's *The Complete Book of Hold'em Poker* is one of the best all-around introductions to hold'em and playing limit poker. David Sklansky and Mason Malmuth have written what many players consider to be the bible of limit hold'em: *Hold'em Poker for Advanced Players: 21st Century Edition.* Because many of your opponents will play exactly how the book suggests, we consider this work essential. Lee Jones's *Winning Low Limit Hold'em* is a superb guide to playing limit hold'em at the low limits. The third edition of his book has three excellent chapters on playing Sit & Go's. Finally, King Yao's *Weighing the Odds in Hold'em Poker* is a great, but more advanced, limit hold'em book.

We're rather biased about books on no-limit hold'em cash games. Our first book, *Mastering No-Limit Hold'em,* is written for the small/restricted buy-in games. If you have a desire to play in an un-limited buy-in no-limit hold'em game, you must read *Pot-Limit & No-Limit Poker* by Stewart Reuben & Bob Ciaffone. In our view, this is the best book on that subject.

Dan Harrington and Bill Robertie have written the two best books on tournament strategy. If you're going to play no-limit hold'em tournaments, make sure you buy *Harrington on Hold'em, Expert Strategy for No-Limit Tournaments, Volume I: Strategic Play and Harrington on Hold'em, Expert Strategy for No-Limit Tournaments, Volume II: The Endgame.*

Mike Caro has written two essential books for any poker player. *The Body Language of Poker: Mike Caro's Book of Tells* shows you how to spot tells and what they mean. *Caro's Fundamental Secrets of Winning Poker* is another great book that covers a wide array of poker games and topics. John Feeney's *Inside the Poker Mind* delves even deeper into the psychology of poker.

David Sklansky's *The Theory of Poker* is not an easy read, but much of the material in this book is excellent, especially the Fundamental Theorem of Poker; we strongly recommend it. Sklansky's *Getting the Best of It* is another excellent text, especially the first few chapters dealing with probability.

If you're going to play poker seriously, you've entered the customer service business. A great book on customer service is Bill Fromm and Len Schlesinger's *The Real Heroes of Business - And Not a CEO Among Them.*

There are three computer software programs that we consider for everyone and two other programs for specific situations. First, go to www.brecware.com/Software/software.html and download Steve Brecher's *Hold'em Showdown.* This program computes the odds for hand confrontations and is a wonderful tool. And you can't complain about the price: it's free. There are versions for both the Mac and Windows.

Then go to www.pokerstove.com and download Andrew Prock's *PokerStove*. This is a simulation tool that allows you to take a hand and compare it to a range of hands. This software readily facilitates "what-if" analysis and has immensely helped our games.

Another excellent piece of software is Mike Caro's *PokerProbe*. This is a DOS-based simulation tool useful when taking one hand (e.g. AA) and seeing what your odds are versus multiple callers.

If you play on the Internet, you should consider purchasing *Poker Tracker* (available at www.pokertracker.com). This software allows you to download hands, learn about your betting patterns, your opponent's patterns, and much more. We highly recommend it.

Finally, if you're not keeping track of your results (with a diary), there is software available that does the job, and does it well. Our choice is ConJelCo's *StatKing*. This Windows-based package allows you to calculate you win rate, confidence, standard deviation and a lot more.

Bibliography

Caro, Mike. *The Body Language of Poker: Mike Caro's Book of Tells*. Secaucus, NJ: Carol Publishing Group, 1984.

———. *Caro's Fundamental Secrets of Winning Poker (Third Edition)*. New York: Cardoza Publishing, 2002.

Carson, Gary. *The Complete Book of Hold'em Poker*. New York: Kensington Publishing Group, 2001.

Ciaffone, Bob and Stewart Reuben. *Pot-Limit & No-Limit Poker*. Self-published. 1997.

Feeney, John, Ph.D. *Inside the Poker Mind*. Henderson, NV: Two Plus Two Publishing, 2000.

Fox, Russell and Scott T. Harker. *Mastering No-Limit Hold'em*. Pittsburgh, PA: ConJelCo, 2005.

Fromm, Bill and Leonard A. Schlesinger. *The Real Heroes of Business – And Not a CEO Among Them*. New York: Doubleday, 1993.

Harrington, Dan and Bill Robertie. *Harrington on Hold'em, Expert Strategy for No-Limit Tournaments, Volume I: Strategic Play*. Henderson, NV: Two Plus Two Publishing, 2004.

———. *Harrington on Hold'em, Expert Strategy for No-Limit Tournaments, Volume II: The Endgame*. Henderson, NV: Two Plus Two Publishing, 2005.

Jones, Lee. *Winning Low-Limit Hold'em (Third Edition)*. Pittsburgh, PA: ConJelCo, 2005.

Simon, S. J. *Why You Lose at Bridge*. New York: Simon and Schuster, 1946. Reprinted by Devyn Press (Louisville, KY), 1994.

Sklansky, David. *The Theory of Poker*. Las Vegas: Two Plus Two Publishing, 1994.

————. *Getting the Best of It*. Henderson, NV: Two Plus Two Publishing, 1997.

Sklansky, David and Mason Malmuth. *Hold'em Poker for Advanced Players: 21st Century Edition*. Henderson, NV: Two Plus Two Publishing, 1999.

Tenner, Mark and Lou Krieger. *Winning Omaha 8 Poker*. Pittsburgh, PA: ConJelCo, 2003.

West, Roy. *Seven-Card Stud: The Complete Course in Winning at Medium and Lower Limits*. New York: Cardoza, 2004.

Yao, King. *Weighing the Odds in Hold'em Poker*. Las Vegas: Pi Yee Press, 2005.

Zee, Ray. *High-Low-Split Poker Seven-Card Stud and Omaha Eight-or-Better for Advanced Players*. Las Vegas: Two Plus Two Publishing, 1994.

Index,
Authors,
Publisher

Index

About the Authors

Russell Fox began playing poker while in college at Berkeley but did not begin to take the game seriously until 1999. Then, while living in Seattle with free time, he began to play in the local cardrooms and tournaments. Almost immediately he became a winning player, and he has not had a losing year to date. He has had numerous final table appearances, including winning the 2001 BARGE no-limit hold'em championship. You can usually find Russ playing no-limit hold'em in one of the Southern California cardrooms.

Away from the tables, Russ is an Enrolled Agent (a Federally licensed tax preparer) and the principal of his own consulting and tax practice, Clayton Financial and Tax. He also has written articles for two poker websites, www.pokerschoolonline.com and www.thepokerforum.com.

Russ's other interests include bicycling and tournament bridge. He resides in Irvine, California.

Scott T. Harker has also been playing poker since college, where poker became an outlet for his competitive juices. He began playing poker seriously to supplement his income while living in Las Vegas. Today Scott plays mainly online poker, in middle-limit and no-limit hold'em cash games, pot-limit Omaha and no-limit hold'em tournaments. Scott has been a successful winning cash game player since 1999.

Scott is the Senior Writer for a legal collections technology firm based in New Jersey, specializing in technical and business documentation. He is also an editor for ConJelCo, and a published poet. Currently living in Youngstown, Ohio, Scott's other interests revolve around his family: his wife Brittania and his son Blaine.

Russell and Scott are the authors of *Mastering No-Limit Hold'em*, which focuses on small/restricted buy-in cash games.

211

About the Publisher

ConJelCo specializes in books and software for the serious gambler. ConJelCo publishes books by Lee Jones, Russ Fox, Scott Harker, Roy Cooke, John Bond, Bill Chen, Jerrod Ankenman, Lou Krieger, Mark Tenner, Kalthleen Keller Watterson, and Dan Paymar. ConJelCo also publishes software including *Blackjack Trainer* for the Macintosh and Windows, *Ken Elliott's CrapSim* for DOS, and *StatKing* for Windows (record keeping software).

We periodically publish a newsletter sent free to our customers. *The Intelligent Gambler* carries articles by our authors as well as other respected authors in the gambling community. In addition, it is the source of information about new ConJelCo products and special offers.

We also sell books, software and videos from other publishers. If you'd like a free catalog or to be put on the mailing list for *The Intelligent Gambler* you can write to us at:

ConJelCo
1460 Bennington Ave.
Pittsburgh, PA 15217

Our phone number is 800-492-9210 (412-621-6040 outside of the U.S.), and our fax number is 412-621-6214.

ConJelCo, and its catalog, is on the Web at *http://www.conjelco.com* or e-mail us at *orders@conjelco.com*.